RIVER
PLAINS
AND
SEA
COASTS

RICHARD J. RUSSELL

RIVER
PLAINS
AND
SEA
COASTS

UNIVERSITY OF CALIFORNIA PRESS
BERKELEY AND LOS ANGELES · 1967

The materials in this book were originally presented as four
lectures on the Charles M. and Martha Hitchcock Foundation
Professorship at the University of California, Berkeley, in 1965.

UNIVERSITY OF CALIFORNIA PRESS
Berkeley and Los Angeles, California

CAMBRIDGE UNIVERSITY PRESS
London, England

244356

FOREWORD

The Hitchcock Lectures, begun at the University of California in Berkeley in 1909, have been unrestricted as to their "scientific or practical" range except that they are not to be "for the advantage of any religious sect, nor upon political subjects." They are public, annual, usually a single series by a scholar from other parts. The Earth Sciences had early attention in the lectures of Harry Fielding Reid on earthquakes and in those on vertebrate evolution by Henry Fairfield Osborn. In later years a half dozen series have been concerned with aspects of the history of the earth and the organic and physical processes that are expressed in its changing face. The Russell lectures of 1965, here published, are the first to take features of land and sea as their theme, a subject now known as geomorphology and which in earlier days and with different emphasis was considered a part of physiography or physical geography.

The appointment of Richard Russell as Professor on the Hitchcock Foundation had several good reasons. He has been a principal in revitalizing geomorphology, giving it new directions, new and sharper means of inspection, and linking it to other disciplines. It was hoped that in meeting the obligation of the lectures he would give an overview of the several lines of inquiry he has followed, their interrelation, results, and prospects. He has done so with a synthesis and perspective and simplicity that will reward any reader who is attentive to the features of land, stream, or seacoast. Also, it was proper to bring him back to the place where he spent his formative years and from which he went out to a life. of greatly independent discovery.

In the twenties the doctrine of William Morris Davis prevailed in all countries of English speech: that the surfaces of the land were to be explained by cycles of erosion, characterized by stages proceeding from youth to old age. The system had the elegance of attractive models that were proposed as representing the stage to which any given land surface would be assigned. By accepting premises and presumed criteria, attention to event and process in actual (geological) time was excluded. Landforms were thus taken out of the context of earth history.

When Professor Davis retired from Harvard University he moved to California, repeatedly lecturing at Berkeley. Here the young Russell became companion to the old master of physiography and here also he began to have doubts that the Davisian doctrine was adequate or even valid. His Hitchcock Lectures begin with the influence of Davis and how he found his independence by moving to Louisiana in 1928. This base, with which he has chosen to remain, gave him a great new field of study, beginning with the Mississippi River, its flood plain and delta. Its terraces led to new insights into the course of glacial and later time in lower latitudes. The Gulf Coast plain with its shores and shallow waters came into his widening range of inquiry, as did alluvial valleys in other continents. Finally his Coastal Studies Institute has engaged in work in the morphology of the borders of sea and land about the world.

This is the record and reading of the forty-year trail of discovery Russell has followed, told in sequence and thus also partly autobiographical. It tells of observations at first casually noted, becoming significant clues, and continued to new understanding of forms and processes. Meanders, levees, terraces that disappear below the flood plain; deltas that are continuing accumulations of sediment and which do not grow as to extent of surface; shapes of lagoons and beaches; beach rock and coral strand and reef—these are some of the items he discusses here. His assurances to the reader that geomorphology is an exciting science in its infancy are substantiated by the new vistas he opens on the nature and origin of lowlands and fringing seas.

CARL SAUER

CONTENTS

1 / ALLUVIAL MORPHOLOGY

WHEN I ENTERED Hayward Union High School in 1910, seven teachers, two of whom were classicists, were intrusted with the secondary education of eighty-seven students. Before graduation in 1914, I had taken a course in physical geography. In fact, I became so interested in the subject that when the summer vacation came I drove my teacher, Dr. Frederick P. Johnson, up to Mt. Lassen to witness the volcanic eruptions that were then in progress.

High schools have become enormous today, and they are many times as numerous, but it is exceptional to find one that offers a course in physical geography. Why the earlier popularity of the subject, as indicated by its having been taught in the then small town of Hayward, California? The textbook used in the course suggests the answer. It was written by William Morris Davis and was first published in 1902.

DAVISIAN PHYSIOGRAPHY

Davis, who retired from his Sturgis-Hooper professorship at Harvard, in 1912, after thirty-five years tenure, remained alert and active until his death a few days prior

to his eighty-fourth birthday, in 1934. His impact on
American geography was revolutionary. Almost single-
handedly, he popularized the subject at all educational
levels.

As a young man, Davis traveled widely. It was said
that he started on new expeditions before the dust of his
last adventure had left his boots. A wealth of field experience, which extended as far as central Asia, resulted in
many journal articles that were characterized by a rigorous presentation of observations and their meticulously
logical interpretation. The most widely known of these
were published during a period of about twenty years,
centering around 1900 (Davis, 1909). His physiographic
essays had the impact of establishing "the American
School of Geography." But during this period he was also
writing many educational essays, such as "The Teaching
of Geography" in 1892 and "Geography in Grammar and
Primary Schools" in 1893. With the enthusiasm of a zeal-
ous missionary he attended and lectured to academic
assemblages ranging in level from modest institutes of
elementary school teachers to the most renowned scientific societies, both at home and abroad. These efforts
resulted in establishing physical geography courses
throughout the nation in universities and even in the
smaller schools in California.

When I took my first geography course at the University of California, in 1917, its content was strictly Davisian physiography. In 1921, when I wrote a syllabus for
the introductory course in physical geography, all map
exercises were based on selections from the 100 United
States Geological Survey quadrangles designated by
Davis as illustrating physiographic features. But few
universities today offer courses in Davisian physiography.

Why did the dominating influence of Davis wane during about the same number of decades that had established it so firmly? For one thing, it was too restrictive in

being concerned with only a narrow segment of geography. Europeans had been developing the discipline on a
much broader base. The explanatory description of landforms was a highly meritorious Davisian technique, but
it degenerated into a game with rigid ground rules. At its
worst, superficial field observations were subjected to de-
ductive reasoning that must follow strictly logical routes
to arrive at physiographic conclusions and generaliza-
tions. At a time before the dawn of rigorous statistical
analyses, aided by the use of electronic computers, there
was insufficient thought given to the idea, "garbage in—
garbage out." In playing the physiographic game an in-
vestigator should draw one or more block diagrams to
illustrate a proposed scheme of sequential landform development. Perhaps the most extreme expression of the
Davisian system was the "pure morphology" of the British. Here the strictest rules existed. All reasoning must
be based on form alone. Any evidence from pedology,
paleontology, hydrology, geophysics, or other outside
disciplines was excluded. Bore-hole evidence was
strictly taboo. Fortunately, this extreme position is being rejected today by most of the younger British geomorphologists.

Davisian physiography introduced a multitude of definitions and developed a jargon that became elaborated
well beyond the vocabularies of the scientists who started
it while describing their exciting geomorphological discoveries when exploring routes for transcontinental rail-
roads or taking inventories and assessing land values in
little known parts of the United States. These men were
coming into direct contact with novel topographic features in the American West. From Clarence King, Major
J. W. Powell, G. K. Gilbert, and others, Davis adopted
many excellent and useful terms, but he and his disciples
went on to develop such elaborate terminologies that
their memorization eventually became less and less justified. Davis stated frequently, "If it is a thing, it deserves

a name." He and his followers were finding new "things" at a fantastic rate during the first two decades of the present century. An explanatory description game might be won by a conclusion such as some stream flowing down a mountain front was consequent, with an obsequent extension; that some landscape had just passed the stage of early maturity; or by proposing several new definitions. Elegance in logic commonly outweighed the presentation of sound field observations.

Having been nurtured in the Davisian School, I naturally selected the Donaldsonville, Louisiana, quadrangle as the example of "old age" topography in my syllabus of 1921. To attain such flatness, it seemed obvious that whatever landforms had existed previously the Mississippi River had succeeded in erasing. After mountains or hills had been worn away, the river faced little in the way of new challenges and now, old and tired, wandered aimlessly on its flood plain. Although in part developed after the river had reached senility, the flood plain was not correctly explained by Davis and his disciples, who supposed that in swinging back and forth it had removed all relief features, accomplished the lateral planation of underlying bedrock, and had increased the distance between its valley walls. These great accomplishments supposedly were hidden because in the wake of its shifting channels the river had deposited a thin veneer of alluvium.

Of course I could not know then that I would become a permanent resident of Louisiana by 1928, nor could I anticipate the physiographic shocks that lay ahead for me. After I had made the move to Louisiana State University and Davis became aware of it, he wrote, "Russell, try to find out why the Mississippi has such a straight channel below New Orleans." This request from an old friend, probably more than anything else, focused my attention on the flood plain and delta of the Lower Mississippi River. But to one accustomed to field work in

California and the Great Basin, Louisiana was flat, uninteresting, and too water-logged to excite immediate
interest. Its moccasins lacked the charitable warning de-
vice of the rattlesnake.

The fact that Davis asked this specific question illustrates the point that even when far advanced in age, he
continued to pose interesting, imaginative problems and
yearned for their solutions. That physiography dropped
out of high school curricula, declined as a field within
university geography departments, and lost ground as its
research values diminished, was more related to the in-
adequacies of his successors than to the shortcomings of
Davis himself. His first-generation students attracted few
disciples. Second-generation students tended to strike
out in new directions, to develop a more meaningful geo-
morphogeny and geomorphology. The "American School
of Physiography" declined at home, but for some decades
prospered abroad.

EARLY LOUISIANA EXPERIENCES

The flood of 1927 convinced nearly everyone that faulty
practices had been advocated by Humphreys and Abbot
in a *Report upon the Physics and Hydraulics of the Mississippi River*, in 1861. Faith in the "bible" of the river
engineers was badly shaken. When it became nakedly
apparent that their "hold by levees" policy had not succeeded in preventing serious floods, the United States
Army Corps of Engineers realized the necessity of trying
new methods. This led to hurried topographic mapping
by the Mississippi River Commission of the Lower Mississippi flood plain, on a scale of approximately one mile
to the inch. The map was compiled from the finest aerial
photography of the day, with ingenious and adequate
ground control. These maps established a new standard
in representing floodplain features because the topogra-
phers who assisted in making them had greater familiar-

ity and longer experience with stream channels and alluvial deposits than those of other mapping agencies. Within about four years all parts of Louisiana subject to Mississippi River flooding were mapped, a feat that was believed impossible by persons accustomed to contemporary methods and rates of issuing detailed topographic maps. To me, a recent resident of a state where maps had been wholly inadequate, the Mississippi River Commission quadrangles were exciting. The Engineers' maps were followed by planimetric quadrangles issued by the United States Geological Survey in cooperation with the state of Louisiana. Soon came the T-sheets of the Coast and Geodetic Survey, an extremely accurate planimetric map of the delta and adjacent coastal flats on a scale of 1:20,000. Some years later the Geological Survey began producing large-scale quadrangles with contour intervals of five feet and less.

The appearance of these maps stimulated Louisiana State University geographers and geologists to investigate some flat, presumably uninteresting, water-logged territory. With Fred Kniffen, I made excursions into the swamps to collect Indian artifacts. This led to a new way of life and my discovery that alluvial morphology is an exciting field of research. My first paper based on Louisiana field work appeared in 1933, its title, "Larto Lake, an Old Mississippi River Channel." The content was somewhat daring at the time because I identified the lake and several others on the flood plain as abandoned river channels of no great antiquity even though they were many miles removed from the active course of the river.

Reestablishment of the Louisiana Geological Survey in 1931 and the new T-sheets made it possible to study the coastal marshes with considerable thoroughness. My earliest studies were in the southwestern part of the state, where Henry V. Howe introduced me to using evidence from bore holes (Pl. 1) (Howe, Russell and McGuirt, 1935). We arrived at the conclusion that the outlet of the

PLATE 1. Extracting a core of sediment underlying a marsh in southwestern Louisiana.

Mississippi into the Gulf of Mexico had shifted widely from time to time and that with those changes came alternations between local coastal advance and retreat. On the whole, the shoreline had advanced gulfward as much as thirty miles during an interval that we regarded as about 2000 years long, but we thought that during something like 95 percent of the time, the coast was retreating landward.

At the time of our investigations we found that on some parts of the coast the retreat was progressing at the rate of 600 feet per century. During such periods, gulf waves transported the coarsest sediments and debris available to them landward to form beaches. These were composed mainly of coarse silt, fine sand, and shell. Episodes of coastal advance, we postulated, occurred when the mouth of the Mississippi River occupied a western position, providing sediment to be deposited along the shore. Old beaches which had been driven landward during a

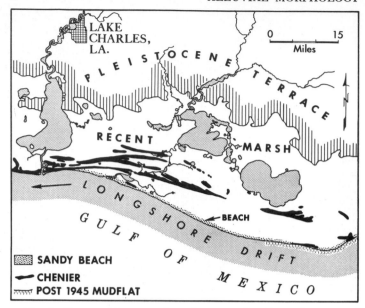

Fig. 1. Geomorphic map of southwestern Louisiana; locations of major cheniers and the mudflat that began to form after 1945.

preceding period of coastal retreat retained their locations after times when surplus sediment arrived on their gulfward sides, leaving them in an inland position (Fig. 1). The deposits in front of them readily became salt marsh (Pl. 2). We accepted the local name for the abandoned beaches—low ridges of sand and shell—and introduced the term *chenier* into scientific literature (Russell and Howe, 1935).

Little did Howe and I realize that we would live to witness another change from western Louisiana coastal retreat to a time when marshes again would advance seaward. I noticed initiation of the process in 1947, when a new mudflat began to appear along the coast. By 1953, members of the staff of the Coastal Studies Institute studied the new accumulation in detail and issued a report based on twenty-two instrumental survey sections between the inner side of the beach and the outer limits of mud accumulation (Morgan, van Lopik and Nichols,

PLATE 2. Live oak *(chêne)* on the gulfward side of an abandoned beach (chenier) fronted by a wide coastal marsh.

1953). The new mudflat, we concluded, was related to the fact that the Atchafalaya River by 1945 had succeeded in filling the lakes of its basin to such a degree that sediment was beginning to reach the Gulf of Mexico in considerable quantity (Fig. 2). The Atchafalaya had augmented its volume during every decade between 1860 and 1950 by taking an increasing percentage of Mississippi River flow. Its discharge at time of flood eventually became more than a quarter of that in the main river channel (Fisk, 1952). Waxing flow resulted in enlarging the Atchafalaya channel to meet increasing discharge requirements and had favored capturing of most of the sedimentary load of Red River, the last downstream major Mississippi tributary. The gradient of the upper part of the Atchafalaya is much steeper than that along the Mississippi, but farther south it becomes quite flat. This lower region had been a large lake that filled the southern part of a basin bounded on the west and south by a ridge

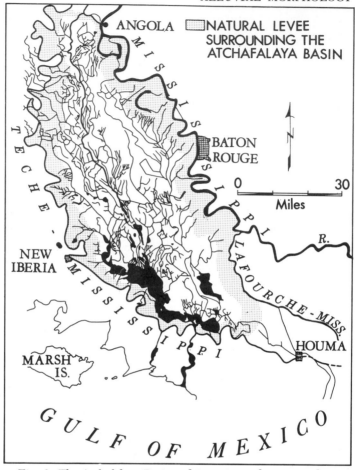

Fig. 2. The Atchafalaya Basin and its major outlets across the confining natural levees of the ancient Teche-Mississippi.

of high land (natural levee) along an old course of the Mississippi now in part followed by Bayou Teche, and a similar ridge along another old Mississippi course now followed by Bayou Lafourche. For many centuries this old Lake Atchafalaya has been dividing into parts that are being shoaled and replaced by new alluvial land (Russell, 1938).

Between 1927 and 1950 some parts of the lower Atchafalaya Basin were alluviated by deposits up to twenty feet thick. A curious example of this occurred northeast of New Iberia, in the western part of the basin. An elaborate hunting and fishing camp had been protected by a surrounding dike about ten feet high. Within ten years the building stood in a pit as deep as the dike and within twenty years the entire site was buried beneath about twenty feet of silt.

Of the two outlets of the Atchafalaya Basin (Fig. 2) the western is artificial and the eastern natural (Lower Atchafalaya River). It was through these that silt, clay, and ooze crossed the Teche natural levee barrier and was transported to the Gulf of Mexico, to be carried west, beyond Marsh Island, to accumulate as the mudflat noticed in 1947. By 1953 the new mudflat had advanced to the position shown at the right in Figure 1. The western end of the accumulation was used as a harbor by shrimp boats seeking protection from easterly winds and became known as the "Mud Hole." Interviews with shrimpers invariably resulted in a precise location for this harbor, but the place identified varied according to the date of the last visit by the informant. At its eastern end the surface of the mudflat, essentially at gulf level, had a width of 100 yards or more in 1953. The offshore deposit extended out across the bottom more than three times that distance as a rule and in places was up to 7 feet thick. At Chenier au Tigre, the most easterly chenier shown in Figure 1, where conditions were particularly favorable to the accumulation of drifting mud the flat had become 1500 feet wide by 1963, completely ruining an active recreation area. Near the shore *Spartina* (couch grass) became established on the mudflat within five years and *Salicornia* (glasswort) and *Juncus* (black rush), typical pioneers of an advancing salt marsh, soon followed. The active beach of 1945 was being converted into a chenier, a process that had advanced westward nearly 90 miles by 1953 and by now well over 120 miles, confirming our explanation of chenier origin.

THE LOWER DELTA

With some initiation in southwestern Louisiana into problems of coastal marshes and fledgling ability in skills such as walking the floating marsh and obtaining information from bore holes, I next sought the answer to Davis' inquiry and began a study of the Lower Mississippi River Delta, publishing the findings in a report (Russell, 1936).

Instead of a comparatively simple problem of differentiating active, dormant, and abandoned channels, together with identifying top-set, fore-set, and bottom-set layers of sediment, the delta study turned out to involve structural geology and led to interpretations that were unpopular among geophysicists of the day. Similarities between the small deltas studied by Gilbert around the shores of Lake Bonneville (Gilbert, 1890) and the huge delta in Louisiana were less impressive than I anticipated. It became evident that I was dealing with a large three-dimensional problem, but fortunately the region was one where many oil wells had been drilled, providing an abundance of cores, cuttings, and driller's logs.

In 1931, Howe and Moresi had estimated the thickness of the post-Jurassic section of southern Louisiana as 27,700 feet and noted that it attained a depth more than twice that of the Sigsbee Deep, the lowest part of the floor of the Gulf of Mexico (Howe and Moresi, 1932). They stated the probability that their estimate was conservative, possibly by 10,000 feet. While they described the geosynclinal structure of the sedimentary accumulation, it remained for Barton, Ritz, and Hickey (1933) to introduce into print Howe's oft-used name for the feature, the Gulf Coast Geosyncline (Fig. 3). At present, geologists ordinarily estimate the thickness of the fill as 50,000 feet, which is well over four times the maximum depth of the Gulf of Mexico (Atwater, 1959). Everyone

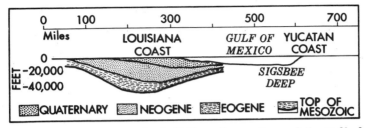

Fig. 3. Section across the Gulf Coast Geosyncline and the Gulf of Mexico (modified, after Atwater).

agrees that the entire sedimentary section accumulated in shallow water, hence on a subsiding floor.

An explanatory description of the Lower Delta had to take into account the fact that the formation of the geosyncline is in active progress. Although geophysicists resisted the idea, it appeared most reasonable to believe that the regional subsidence of the delta and its surroundings is a direct result of sedimentary loading. To the argument, "you cannot sink a barge by loading it with feathers," meaning that the addition of lighter-weight sediments at the surface could not displace heavier basement rock, came the reply, "although the earth's crust has considerable tensional and compressional strength in resisting horizontal stresses, it yields readily to vertical stresses such as are being imposed by accumulating sediment." Water in lake basins or glacial caps of ice on continents is certainly much lighter than sedimentary rock, yet definitely it has depressed the crust in many cases. The delta, as a "barge," was being sunk and we felt that it would be more useful for geophysicists to explain the mechanism, rather than to deny a fact.

Gilbert, in 1890, had shown that the weight of water in Lake Bonneville when removed, permitted the central part of the basin to rise about 168 feet. Relief from Pleistocene ice load explains active uplift in Scandinavia and many other areas. In the vicinity of Uppsala, Sweden, the current rate of uplift is on the order of half a meter per century, near the head of the Gulf of Bothnia it is one meter, and it may be considerably faster in eastern Canada. Shorelines of no great antiquity and Viking barrows are highly elevated in Scandinavia and manor houses a few centuries old that originally were built on low islands surrounded by protective marshes now stand on low eminences above dry grain fields. The dryness of extensive areas surrounding the Isle of Ely is undoubtedly related to slow upward rebound of the area in response to the disappearance of late-Pleistocene ice cover, although credit should not be denied the Dutch engineers for initiating reclamation of the English Fens.

Among my initial shocks when investigating the Mississippi Delta was the discovery that its land area has remained essentially constant since the date of the first reliable surveys. Active passes were advancing into the Gulf of Mexico at rapid rates, and in many cases water from six to nine feet deep in bays between them had been filled in a few years, but all such increases in land area had been counterbalanced by losses caused by erosion and subsidence of land in parts of the delta removed from areas receiving alluvial deposits from active channels. The record of a century indicated essential constancy in land area.

A very accurate map by Professor S. H. Lockett, probably dating from 1872, indicates a true "bird-foot" shape of the Lower Delta. All of the bays, excepting only East Bay, between Southwest and South Passes, now have been at least partially filled, so the original talons of the foot are webbed, converting the foot almost into that of a duck (Fig. 4). The shank of the leg has been considerably widened along most of the river course. On the other hand, to counterbalance these increases in land area, there have been erosional losses along the east coast of the delta and subsidence that has lowered land used agriculturally a century ago, so that it has become wet marsh.

Another shock was to find that instead of Gilbert's universally accepted tripartite division of stratigraphic units

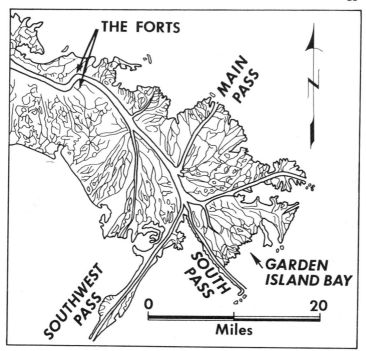

Fig. 4. Lower Delta of the Mississippi River.

into top-set, fore-set, and bottom-set beds, the most important lithologic contrasts occur in directions about at
right angles to those of stream courses. In the delta, as
upstream on the flood plain, sorting of sediments exhibits sharp contrasts in short distances away from stream
channels, whereas there is relative uniformity for great
distances up- or down-stream. Gradation into finer sizes
is conspicuous between the coarser sediments of natural
levee crests, finer grains on levee backslopes, and the clay
or ooze deposits of the basins between levees. If but three
lithologic units are to be designated in the delta the most
significant choice would recognize the coarse sediments
along stream channels, the fine and generally organic deposits of basins, and, out in front of the delta, prodelta
clay. When a pass grows seaward its natural levee deposits cover prodelta clay, creating a condition favorable

to upward, diapiric clay intrusions, forming small topographic mounds, called mudlumps (Morgan, Coleman,
and Gagliano, 1963). The natural levee deposits are so
restricted to channels and their immediate flanks that in
deltas they now are called "bar-finger sands (Fisk, 1961).

Differentiation between kinds of subsidence became a

PLATE 3. John Huner, Jr., former state geologist of Louisiana,
gaining experience in walking through tall "cutgrass."

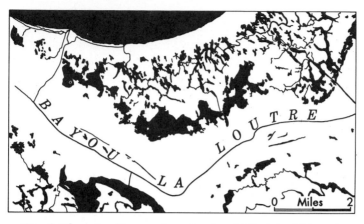

Fig. 5. The natural levees of an abandoned Mississippi River channel east of New Orleans are firm and dry, but large ponds occur in levee-flank depressions.

problem in the Lower Delta. One kind became altogether too apparent during our early field work. We encountered a firm surface when walking along the natural levees even of the smallest channels. Walking across basins, the grassy marsh was a somewhat difficult problem at first, but a person acquires skill in judging footings and, in time, gains the ability almost instantaneously to come up with an alternative if some grassy clump appears more firm than proves to be the case when stepped upon. Where tall "cutgrass" prevents good vision an additional complication is introduced (Pl. 3). The main problem, however, arose between the margins of a marsh and the backslopes of natural levees, both along active and abandoned channels. Here are "levee-flank depressions," some of which are ponded for long distances and all much less firm than surfaces on either side (Fig. 5). To cross them one might have to "swim the hyacinth or alligator weed." The technique involved is a combination of swimming and crawling over a mat of floating vegetation. These depressed areas follow channel bends faithfully and are the direct result of the load imposed by natural levees, involving local subsidence either by compaction of underlying sediments or their lateral displacement.

Another kind of subsidence, more regional in character, was described by Eugene A. Smith in 1894 in the
vicinity of Mobile Bay, Alabama (Smith, Johnson, and
Langdon, 1894). He noted what in effect were changes
that affected the diets of prehistoric Indians. As sites of
occupance subsided, their surroundings became increasingly saliné and the dominant shells of middens changed
from fresh- to salt-water clams, from *Unio*, through *Ran-
gia*, to *Ostrea*. Although by our standards the tastiness of
the food supply increased, the dry area suitable for hab-
itation diminished. In more recent years, William Mc-
Intire has examined the question of Indian sites in extreme detail (McIntire, 1954). The middens and mounds
have experienced various degrees of regional subsidence.
This is a characteristic of all deltas and marshes along the
Gulf Coast.

Using evidence from borings we found, early in our
delta studies, that a large Indian mound presses down on
an uncertain foundation so that its central part commonly sinks to a depth of up to two or three feet below
its margins. In most cases the margins themselves also
have subsided (Fig. 6). The majority of mounds are com-

Fig. 6. Indian mound on a natural levee depressed underlying silt
and shares in regional subsidence accompanied by thickening marsh
sediments.

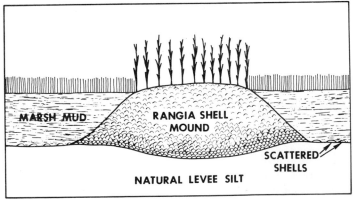

posed of clam shells. They are located either on submerged natural levee crests or the relatively firm shores
of lakes. That these features have subsided is demonstrated by the fact that shells washed from a mound
occur under a cover of marsh deposits in decreasing frequency with increased distance across its foundation on
natural levee or lakeshore sediments. The foundation
datum remains essentially constant in elevation for considerable distances. Over distances such as ten miles or
more along a buried channel the basement upon which
mounds were built may vary between an elevation from
above sea level to ten feet and more below, increasing
in depth seaward. Much of this evidence comes from
abandoned deltas east and northeast of New Orleans, the
area where details of regional subsidence are known in
greatest detail.

Near the active mouths of the Mississippi we learned
that subsidence varies considerably within short distances, as shown by rates established by United States
Army Engineers bench marks. Although the evidence is
not completely trustworthy, a reasonable interpretation
suggests that near Burrwood, toward the end of the most
active channel, Southwest Pass, the rate is about 8 feet
per century. At the mouth of less active South Pass it is
about six feet and at Head of Passes, somewhat over
twenty miles inland, it amounts to only twenty inches.
These observations indicate a direct relationship between subsidence and deposition rates. On a wider regional scale, this is also shown by the eastward slope of
the Recent-Pleistocene contact, which normally lies
within 15 or 20 feet below sea level along the coast in
stable western Louisiana but appears to reach a depth
of at least 700 feet near the southern part of the delta
(Fisk and McFarlan, 1955). Kolb and van Lopik (1958)
estimate a value of more than 900 feet.

To most Gulf Coast geologists, it appears apparent
that the continuing contribution of load of the Missis-

sippi and other rivers builds their deltas downward rather than areally. While there has been a considerable increase in land area resulting from the growth of the deltaic coastal plain during the last 3,000 years, in most of the area affected the deposit has been thin. During this time the deposits that have accumulated in and near deltas have become astonishingly thick. I have compared the base of the Recent Mississippi alluvium with the shape of a ladle, the deep bowl of which centers in the delta region and the handle of which extends up the Lower Mississippi Valley (Russell, 1940). Bernard and Leblanc (1965) believed that the Quaternary deposits in the bowl are at least 2,000 feet thick. The ladle shape, we found, is also characteristic of Pleistocene equivalents of the Lower Delta. If we turn to the deposits in the Gulf Coast Geosyncline that have accumulated during the last 185 million years, we find a record of a long succession of coalescing deltas, with notable lenticular thickening at various places below the coastal plain. The process of geosynclinal development started south of the Ouachitas and the axis of the structure in time migrated across the state of Louisiana to its present position approximately along the coast. Similar history occurred along the coast from south of Tuxpan, Mexico, to the western part of Florida, giving the geosyncline great length. Pronounced "bowl effects" occur in deltas of the Rio Grande and other rivers. It has been estimated that during the Quaternary, a time that began something on the order of two million years ago when the effects of continental ice accumulation were first reflected by fluctuations in sea level, some 10,000 feet of sedimentary section has accumulated at places along the structure.

FIELD WORK DURING THE FISK ERA

Sharper focus on inland problems was initiated after Harold N. Fisk joined the Louisiana Geological Survey. He was soon to become a member of Louisiana State University's School of Geology faculty and later Consultant to the Mississippi River Commission. On his arrival, in 1935, Fisk was thoroughly inoculated with the Davisian ideas of Nevin Fenneman and felt certain that the flood plain of the Lower Mississippi River was the product of lateral corrasion. It was a shock when he learned that the depth of alluvium between valley walls is ordinarily several times deeper than the lowest pools along the river channel. It was an impressive discovery to find that the contact between the base of the Recent alluvium and underlying Pleistocene beds is sharply defined, not only because the alluvium has a graveliferous base but also because nearly all of it exhibits effects of chemical reduction, whereas the uppermost surface of the Pleistocene is conspicuously oxidized (Fig. 7). Most of the fill has remained water-soaked ever since it was deposited but the pre-Recent surface, had been exposed to the atmosphere for a long time and the parts above the water table became oxidized. In places soil profiles were developed to be covered by Recent alluvium.

By 1944, Fisk's monumental *Geological Investigation of the Alluvial Valley of the Lower Mississippi River* appeared. One of its plates indicates the pre-Recent topography of the now-alluvium-filled valley in extreme

Fig. 7. Section based on borings one mile or less apart across the narrowest part of the Lower Mississippi Valley (after Fisk).

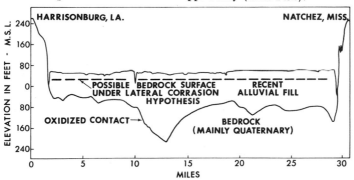

detail. This map was based on evidence from over 60,000 borings. Some five years later it was tested by evidence from 10,000 new borings and not one of its 25-foot contours anywhere in the area between valley walls had to be shifted. The only changes needed today for updating the map occur near the coast, where the alluvium is now known to be at least 367 feet thick, rather than something less than 350.

From projecting the gradient of the pre-Recent Mississippi River between today's valley walls for 100 miles to the then-shoreline, we estimate the pre-Recent stand of sea level at −450 feet (Russell, 1964a). This technique is used because there has been little modification of the gradient within the valley, effects of subsidence and possible compaction of sediments are absent, whereas there has been considerable displacement of the old channel bed for various reasons, including displacements along faults across the coastal marshes and continental shelf. The thalweg gradient between Cairo, Illinois, and the southern limit of valley walls is remarkably uniform, with a slope of 0.83 foot per mile. If to the known depth of 367 feet, 83 is added, the −450 foot stand is established.

Across the 100-mile-wide shelf of western Louisiana, the oxidized Pleistocene surface lies at a depth of about 550 feet, 100 feet of which we attribute to regional subsidence. In Louisiana we regard the beginning of the Recent as the time when sea level started its last major rise, possibly on the order of 80,000 years ago. This usage has the advantage of bounding time periods by changes of stratigraphic significance.

The arrival of Fisk brought a tremendous acceleration in floodplain research. Doctoral dissertations and a flow of publications ensued, many with conclusions too novel to gain wide acceptance among geomorphologists of the time. The Davis-inspired physiographers had thought almost entirely in terms of erosional modification, but in Louisiana we were confronted with landforms of depositional origin. The Donaldsonville quadrangle does not exhibit an old-age surface. It displays part of the largest depositional flat and youngest sedimentary accumulations and landforms of any of the 100 sheets selected by Davis. The width of the Mississippi Valley, from wall to wall, was not the product of lateral corrasion. Rather, it is a result of deposition within a valley cut toward a level established by the last Pleistocene low stand of the sea. Surficial modification of the flood plain is still in progress.

Fisk and I had in common a background of completed Ph.D theses in igneous-rock areas in the Great Basin and we had both been brought up in the Davisian school. Alluvial morphology was new, not only to us, but generally. The bedrock hills we had regarded as small might have a relief of several hundred feet, but in Louisiana we had to make the adjustment of becoming able to recognize contrasts amounting to only a few feet or even inches. True, I had written a 193-page report on the Lower Delta (Russell, 1936), but everyone knew that it was a flat area of depositional origin. In 1938, I wrote another report, 83 pages long, describing the landforms of two inland parishes in which the relief was less than thirty feet in an area of 875 square miles (Russell, 1938). But we entered floodplain investigations essentially as novices and without the benefit of many established research techniques. Useful literature was inadequate, but we had excellent aerial photographs and maps, so we struck out into the unknown.

Among our first conclusions was recognition of the fact that the deep alluvial fill of the Lower Mississippi Valley had been deposited during the last major rise of sea level. We determined the volume of the alluvial fill between Cape Girardeau, Missouri, and the southernmost limits of the valley walls as about 1,000 cubic miles. This round number was regrettable as it suggests a rough estimate, as did the value of 14,500 feet for the elevation of Mt. Whitney, determined by precise leveling some years ago.

A common gag at the time was the suggestion that one foot should have been added or subtracted, "for accuracy." Our value was obtained by a detailed analysis based on Fisk's map of the pre-Recent topography and I firmly believe that if an even more definitive analysis is made at some future date, the 1,000 cubic mile estimate will involve an error of less than 5 percent. Fisk found that the alluvial section could be divided into two parts, a lower, graveliferous part in which almost all samples contained coarse sand and some gravel, and an upper part where they did not, except along some definite trains following now-buried stream courses or in areas near alluvial cones of tributary rivers.

PLEISTOCENE TERRACES

We found the same bipartite division in Pleistocene terrace deposits that Fisk noted in the Recent valley fill. It was somewhat of a shock to find that the terraces were not erosional in origin, but on them we found natural levees, backswamp deposits, and stratigraphic sequences like those in the Recent. With more detailed mapping we found that the deposition of each terrace system was limited to valleys cut in response to some lowered sea level. Eventually we identified four major terrace systems and from that fact concluded that there had been five major Quaternary glacial stages, each of which had dropped sea level appreciably, and interspersed were periods of valley fill, accumulated when meltwaters were causing seas to rise or remain at a level close to that of today. Four of the alluvial sequences were formed during the Pleistocene and the fifth during the Recent (Russell, 1940).

Gulf Coast terrace deposits are both glacial and interglacial in age. The oldest beds in a stratigraphic sequence were the first to be buried toward the outer edge of the continental shelf. Continental glaciation was just passing a peak when they were deposited and sea level was initiating a major rise. As continuing supplies of meltwater reached the ocean basins, the inner edge of a new geological formation worked across the shelf and eventually up estuaries and into valleys, where the alluvium continued to thicken as long as the rise continued. Division of the Quaternary into parts resembling other recognized units in the geological record must be based on alluvial sequences such as these. The oldest beds, unfortunately, lie buried beneath subsequent deposits out on the shelves or in deeper water beyond. The upper parts of an alluvial sequence are visible on land and for the most part were deposited when most continental ice had melted, hence represent interglacial times. Attempts to decipher Quaternary history on evidence of glacial deposits are not likely to be satisfactory for several reasons. The younger deposits probably cover older ones. Moraines, outwash accumulations, and other landforms associated with glacial advances or retreats commonly were severely modified by the advance of all subsequent continental ice sheets. It is from coastal regions and mainly from areas removed from glaciated areas that the true record of Quaternary events is most readily and unequivocally ascertained—from land-sea relationships.

Were valley cutting and filling the only factors involved it would be extremely difficult to differentiate between individual Quaternary formations. Happily, this is not the case. The entire Gulf Coast region has experienced southward tilting throughout the development of the Gulf Coast Geosyncline. The upper surfaces of inland Quaternary terrace formations are now elevated well above sea level, while their gulfward extensions have been lowered to positions where they have been covered by subsequent deposits. Thus a normal stratigraphic sequence is encountered by borings in coastal Louisiana and across the shelf. Inland the formations have attained higher elevations, in proportion to their relative age. The

PLATE 4. The somewhat dissected youngest Pleistocene terrace near the Rhône delta covers most of the picture. The Vistre flood plain of Recent age is shown to the right. Trees in the far distance, both above the terrace, and along the horizon to the right, rise from the Recent coastal marsh that overlies the terrace formation.

latter relationship was known in France at least since 1843, when it was described by Boubée (1843).

There is an intermediate zone of convergence of alluvial surfaces between the inland area where the oldest deposits stand most elevated and the coastal and offshore area where they are most deeply buried. The zone in which the upper surfaces of terrace formations converge with and finally pass beneath younger deposits is from forty to seventy miles wide in southern Louisiana. In the lower Rhône Valley of France it is somewhat less than ten miles wide (Pl. 4) (Russell, 1942). Inland from the zone of convergence (called hingelines by Fisk) terrace surfaces extend up main valleys at levels separated by essentially constant intervals. Between northern Louisiana and the head of the alluvial valley of the Lower Mississippi River, at Cape Girardeau, all terrace surfaces dip downvalley at about the same rate as the Recent flood plain. Near Forrest City, Arkansas, both on the Ozark Front and Crowley Ridge, the elevations of terrace surfaces above the flood plain amount to about 40, 100, 200, and 350 feet. It is thus a comparatively simple matter to identify the deposits associated with each interglacial stage of the Pleistocene.

Another fortunate circumstance associated with Gulf Coast Quaternary terraces, at least between Texas and Alabama in territory most familiar to me, is the fact that many river courses changed locations appreciably between Quaternary intrenchment intervals. Several early Pleistocene tributaries of the Mississippi flowed southward across Kansas and Oklahoma into a valley approximating today's Red River, bringing to Louisiana huge volumes of chert gravel containing Paleozoic fossils. The oldest terrace formation everywhere is characterized by the largest content of gravel. Subsequently the gravel has been reworked and redeposited in all younger terrace formations and in the Recent alluvium. River locations changed appreciably in about mid-Pleistocene times, so that the major channels across the Great Plains assumed eastward rather than southward courses as during the earlier Pleistocene.

The oldest equivalent of White River, in northern Arkansas, occupied a course up to twenty miles south of the ones followed later, along the valley leading past Batesville. The floor of the long abandoned valley today has the same elevation as the surface of the oldest Pleistocene terrace in the vicinity. Three more recent terraces lie at appropriate levels along the sides of the present-day course of White River. In Louisiana, the earlier courses of Red River were located a considerable distance east of Shreveport, which is on the river today. By patient mapping of terrace deposits we gradually deciphered considerable Gulf Coast Quaternary history.

The mapping of terraces confronted us with many problems. The first was solved when we recognized their depositional origin and abandoned ideas that they were erosional remnants. Local variations in elevations of undissected terrace surfaces puzzled us until we fully realized the amount of relief that exists on today's flood plain.

New Orleans is a flat city, but its river front lies more
than 20 feet higher than the natural elevation of a considerable area toward Lake Pontchartrain. Bank-full
river stage, which means natural-levee-crest elevation,
of the Mississippi at Baton Rouge is more than 30 feet
higher than the floor of the basin six miles to the west.
Any elevation on a terrace remnant may represent part
of a natural levee, or more probably, some part of a basin
well removed from stream channels. Thus it became necessary to take into account the various facies present on
terrace surfaces, relating each to a range of characteristic
elevations. The worst trap in terrace studies is the snare
of employing precise instrumental surveys while remaining oblivious to the magnitude of original surface irregularities. There is no point in being concerned with
inches or centimeters, or in many cases with intervals of

Fig. 8. Regional elevations (in feet) on the youngest Pleistocene
(Prairie) terrace in Louisiana (after Fisk).

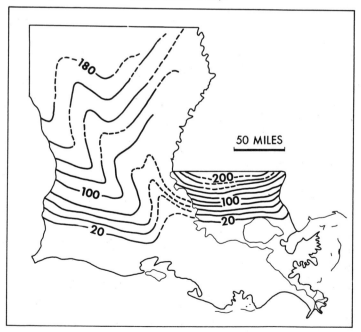

from 5 to 20 feet, when fundamental levels of significant terraces may be from 40 to 350 feet apart vertically.

Fisk employed an excellent technique for determining regional slopes of coastwise and fluvial terraces across areas of considerable size, that is at least 100 miles wide (Fisk, 1942). Large numbers of elevations were determined on undissected terrace surfaces and plotted on a master map. Excluded from consideration were all dissected areas and terraces along minor streams. Once the master map was sufficiently filled with spot elevations, smooth contours were drawn to indicate regional slopes (Fig. 8). These maps are useful in many ways. Bunching or wider spacing of contours, for example, focuses attention on anomalous areas. In this example it will be noted that terrace slope is much steeper in territory north of New Orleans than in western Louisiana. This

Fig. 9. Pleistocene and Tertiary outcrop areas (highly generalized) of Louisiana. In the northwest part of the state the distinction is somewhat difficult to recognize.

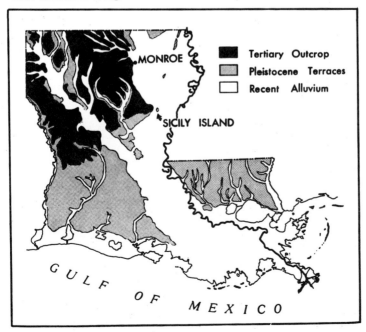

is because the area north of Lake Ponchartrain is experi-
encing active uplift at the present time. The slope shown
is that of the youngest Pleistocene terrace. When maps
showing slopes of the earlier terraces are examined it
becomes apparent that this uplift has been in progress
throughout the Quaternary in this part of Louisiana and
the adjacent part of Mississippi. Location of this area
immediately north of the area of most rapid coastal subsidence, the location of most-active Quaternary deltas,
suggests that isostatic adjustment is taking place; subsidence of the coastal region being compensated by uplift a short distance inland (Russell, 1939). Neither process is more than feebly active in western Louisiana.

Another merit of the regional slope technique is that
the maps provide a basis for distinguishing older terrace
deposits from outcrops of Tertiary rock rising above
regional terrace levels (Fig. 9). Any rock unit that rises
higher than the regional level of a terrace must be older.
In regions other than the Gulf Coast a clue for differentiating between terrace deposits and Tertiary outcrops
might not be particularly useful, but in Louisiana weathering has been so intense, soil development so deep,
vegetational cover so dense, and mass-movement so general that superficially Tertiary outcrops resemble closely

Fig. 10. Sketch of a railroad-cut exposure of undisturbed Tertiary
bedrock and its residual cover, southwest of Monroe in northern Louisiana. The section is about 300 feet long and 30 feet deep.

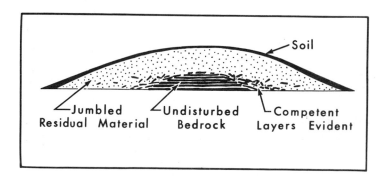

the appearance of older terrace deposits (Fig. 10) (Russell, 1946b). The regional terrace-slope maps are also useful in establishing relationships between major terraces and those along minor streams, even though the latter climb up their valleys to higher than regional levels. Unless downfaulted a tributary-stream terrace cannot be lower than the regional elevation of the major terrace into which it leads.

The ideal terrace map, as far as I know, has never been made. It would start as a geological map in which contact boundaries are indicated between terrace or other rock units as individual formations. Then, in the simplest case, each terrace-formation outcrop would be subdivided into two parts; one showing the area where little or no dissection has occurred, and the other where much or all of the original surface has been lost. The "terrace," *sensu stricto*, is the topographic feature present where minimum dissection has occurred. The dissected surface of the formation could be subdivided in various ways, for example, into areas with contrasting degrees or varieties of dissection. A student at Louisiana State University is preparing a map something like that at the present time, but it shows coastal rather than fluvial terraces and differentiates between barrier, back-barrier, and fluvial facies of deposits and topography.

RECENT ALLUVIAL CONES

As we extended our terrace mapping northward along the Mississippi Valley, we encountered the problem of distinguishing between Pleistocene terraces and the remnants of huge cones of Recent origin leading from valleys of major tributary rivers into the main flood plain (Fig. 11). The cone surfaces superficially appear as flat as terraces and scarps along their sides may rise abruptly from the flood plain for as many as several tens of feet vertically.

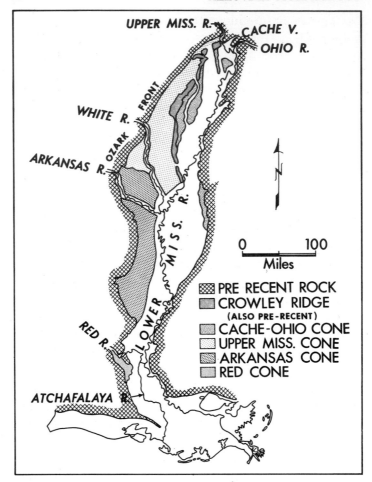

Fig. 11. Recent major alluvial cones of the Lower Mississippi River Valley.

In Louisiana we had a comparatively simple case. Red River, until less than 1,500 years ago, was actively building its flood plain southeastward from Alexandria into the Mississippi Valley to the east of Opelousas. Then, after its cone became sufficiently alluviated to reach an elevation permitting the river to take advantage of a low gap in its eastern valley wall the Red established a new course, leading across a dissected Pleistocene terrace.

The new course reduced to about one quarter the distance required for reaching an elevation on the Mississippi flood plain similar to that along the old course. This increased the river gradient and caused rejuvenation of the Red, so that it began to incise its alluvial cone, leaving a flood plain less than 1,500 years old as a terrace of very recent origin. The incision now extends upstream into Texas and has brought about significant changes. In the vicinity of Shreveport, for example, there was extensive and serious flooding when the Red overtopped its banks in 1908. Although floods in the 1940s brought a greater-than-1908 discharge, no flooding occurred because the incised channel had become deeply cut and its valley walls had widened considerably.

A much more spectacular case of cone abandonment occurred on the Arkansas River below Little Rock. For much of late Recent time the river had been building a large cone that extended south from Pine Bluff for about 175 miles, to the vicinity of Sicily Island, Louisiana, about 225 miles from the mouth of the Arkansas Valley. Later the river was diverted eastward at Pine Bluff and developed a much steeper gradient. This resulted in intrenchment of the original cone for about 50 miles and erosional removal of its eastern part for an additional 150 miles. The scarp indicating the western limit of cone removal is called Maçon Ridge in Louisiana, and its elevation is about forty feet above the Mississippi flood plain near the Arkansas-Louisiana state line. Relict natural levees, remnant channels of Arkansas dimensions, and backswamp basins today dominate the surface of this huge abandoned Recent alluvial cone.

The Mississippi built an impressive cone down its Recent valley to the west of Crowley Ridge. When, less than 3,000 years ago, the river had alluviated its cone high enough to spill across Thebes Gap to join the Ohio near Cairo, the old cone became intrenched by channels of the St. Francis, White, and other rivers.

A cone extending out from the Recent Cache Valley course of the Ohio slopes gently southward for 240 miles to a latitude south of today's junction between the Arkansas and Mississippi rivers. After the Ohio established its present course leading past Paducah, Kentucky, the old cone became severely dissected, but some remnants of its surface remain unaltered, such as the 33-mile-long Sikeston Ridge in Missouri and a flat bench 110 miles long on the eastern side of Crowley Ridge.

Any of these, or many other, cone remnants of Recent origin might be considered as excellent examples of Pleistocene terraces when first encountered. In fact they seemed so to us. But only by detailed mapping, by measurement of slopes which in all instances proved to be steeper than either the local flood plain or regional surfaces of Pleistocene terraces in the vicinity, and by studying stream patterns and surface facies could we positively identify most of the Recent alluvial cones leading into the Lower Mississippi Valley. We were able to follow some of these Recent cones southward by evidence from borings into places where they lie buried under the Recent alluvium of today's Mississippi flood plain.

Recent alluvial cones in the Lower Mississippi Valley are not insignificant features. Their combined area amounts to 15,000 square miles, or almost that of The Netherlands. The area of the active Lower Mississippi flood plain from Cape Girardeau to the end of the valley walls is 22,000 square miles. If the Mississippi deltaic coastal plain is added, the total comes to 35,000, which is nearly the area of Indiana. In comparison, the area covered by Recent cones is nearly 43 percent as extensive.

MAGNITUDE OF QUATERNARY PROBLEMS

An interesting by-product of Quaternary research was the discovery that inversion of topography since the mid-Quaternary is relatively commonplace in the Gulf Coastal Plain (Russell, 1964b). Many of the highest parts

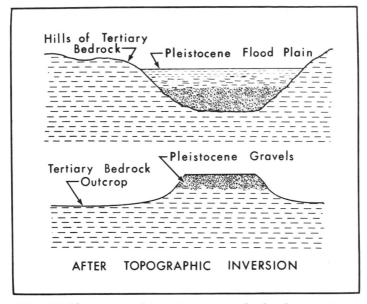

Fig. 12. The process of inverting topography has been active in northwestern Louisiana during the Quaternary.

of Louisiana are gravel-capped. Some adjacent lowlands display Tertiary outcrops. In most cases the gravel caps map out as lower parts of terrace formations. These facts led us to formulate an important generalization: "Whenever you find comparatively extensive gravel outcrops, your first thought should be, 'this was once the bottom of a valley.'" The Tertiary and earlier Pleistocene surface configuration, at least in Louisiana and Mississippi, in many cases has been so completely altered that extensive hills have been reduced to lowlands (Fig. 12). The gravels in valleys between these former hills have protected underlying rocks from erosion, so have preserved the rocks in today's uplands. The scarcity of terraces over much of the state of Mississippi apparently arose because hilly terrain was present over much of the state during most of the Quaternary. The old hilly area has now been reduced to the lowness and relative flatness it has today. Experience in Gulf Coast areas where topographic inversion has occurred so extensively prompted me to suggest the desirability of investigating the possibility of inversion on a wide scale across the Great Plains (Russell, 1958).

Until people are prepared to "think big" enough to comprehend Quaternary geology, many of my suggestions may sound fanciful. But I fully believe that unless a person thoroughly understands problems such as the Quaternary history of Crowley Ridge, the linear upland between the late Pleistocene and early Recent Mississippi and Ohio valleys as far south as Helena, Arkansas, he isn't ready to tackle Pleistocene geomorphology. That particular history, incidentally, involves the erosion of at least 5,000 cubic miles of Quaternary alluvium in territory between the Ozark Front and some as yet undetermined boundary in western Kentucky, Tennessee, and Mississippi and also the deposition of about an equivalent volume of fill during five cycles of incision and subsequent valley filling.

The volume of material eroded from landmasses during each of the low stands of Quaternary seas and that deposited during times of rising sea level is much greater than most geologists and geomorphologists comprehend at the present time. It presents research opportunities offering most interesting conclusions and will lead to quantitative information that geophysicists must take into account.

REFERENCES

Abbot, H. L. (see Humphreys)
Atwater, G. I.
    1959 Geology and petroleum development on the continental shelf of the Gulf of Mexico. Fifth World Petrol. Cong. (Rome), Sec. I, paper 21, 25 pp.
Barton, D. C. (with C. H. Ritz, and M. Hickey)
    1933 Gulf coast geosyncline. Am. Assoc. Petrol. Geols., Bull. 17:1446–1458.

Bernard, H. A. (with R. J. Leblanc)
1965 Résumé of the Quaternary geology of the north-western Gulf of Mexico province, *in* The Quaternary of the United States. Internat. Assn. for Quat. Research, p. 137–185.

Boubée, N.
1843–1847 Sur le creusement des valées à plusieures étages. Soc. Géol. France, Bull. 4:376–380 and 2 ser. 4:825–832.

Coleman, J. M. (see Morgan, 1963)

Davis, W. M.
1909 Geographical essays (D. W. Johnson, ed.), Boston (Ginn and Co.), 777 pp.; reprinted, 1957, New York (Dover Publications). Contains the most widely known of Davis' earlier writings, both physiographic and educational.

Fisk, H. N.
1942 Depositional terrace slopes in Lousiana. Jour. Geomorphol., 2:181–199.
1944 Geological investigation of the alluvial valley of the Lower Mississippi River. U. S. Army, Corps of Engineers, Mississippi River Commission (Vicksburg), 78 pp. + 33 pl.
1952 Geological investigation of the Atchafalay Basin and the problem of Mississippi River diversion. U. S. Army, Corps of Engineers, Mississippi River Commission (Vicksburg), 2 vols., 150 pp. + 59 pl.
1961 Bar-finger sands of the Mississippi Delta, *in* Geomtry of Sandstone Bodies, Tulsa (Am. Assoc. Petrol. Geols.) p. 29–52.
1955 (with E. McFarlan, Jr.) Late Quaternary deltaic deposits of the Mississippi River: local sedimentation and basin tectonics, *in* A. Poldervaart (ed.), Crust of the Earth. Geol. Soc. Am., Spec. Paper 62:279–302.

Gagliano, S. M. (see Morgan, 1963)

Gilbert, G. K.
1890 Lake Bonneville. U. S. Geol. Surv., Monograph 1:xx + 438 pp.

Hickey, M. (see Barton)

Howe, H. V. (see Russell, 1935)
1932 (with C. K. Moresi) Geology of Iberia Parish. La. Dept. Consv., Geol. Surv., Bull. 1:187 pp.

1935 (with R. J. Russell and J. H. McGuirt) Physiography of Southwest Louisiana. La. Dept. Consv., Geol. Surv., Bull. 6:1–72.

Humphreys, A. A.
1861 (with H. L. Abbot) Report upon the physics and hydraulics of the Mississippi River; upon the protection of the alluvial region against overflow; and upon the deepening of the mouths: based upon surveys and investigations, submitted to the Bureau of Topographical Engineers, War Department, 1861. Philadelphia (J. B. Lippincott & Co.), cxivi + 456 pp.

Johnson, L. C. (see Smith)
Kolb, C. R.
1958 (with J. R. van Lopik) Geology of the Mississippi River deltaic plain, Southeastern Louisiana, U. S. Army, Corps of Engineers, Mississippi River Commission (Vicksburg), Waterways Exp. Sta., Tech. Rept. 3–483, 120 pp. + 17 pl.

Langdon, D. W., Jr. (see Smith)
Leblanc, R. J. (see Bernard)
McFarlan, E., Jr. (see Fisk, 1955)
McGuirt, J. H. (see Howe, 1935)
McIntire, W. G.
1954 Correlation of prehistoric settlements and of delta development, Tech. Rept. 5, contract N7onr 35608, 388 002, La. State Univ. and ONR Geography Branch, 65 pp. (available on microfilm, L. S. U. Library).
1958 Prehistoric Indian settlements of the changing Mississippi River Delta. La. State Univ. Press, Univ. Studies, Coastal Studies Series, No. 1, 128 pp. + 33 figs. and 13 foldout maps.

Moresi, C. K. (see Howe, 1932)
Morgan, J. P.
1953 (with J. R. van Lopik and L. G. Nichols) Occurrence and development of mudflats along the western Louisiana coast. Tech. Rept. 2, contract N7onr 35608, 388 002, La. State Univ. and ONR Geography Branch, 34 p. (available on microfilm, L. S. U. Library).
1963 (with J. M. Coleman and S. M. Gagliano) Mudlumps at the mouth of South Pass, Mississippi River.

La. State Univ. Press, Univ. Studies, Coastal Studies
Series, No. 10, xvi + 190 pp.

Nichols, L. G. (see Morgan, 1953)

Ritz, C. H. (see Barton)

Russell, R. J. (see Howe, 1935)

1933 Larto Lake, an old Mississippi River channel. La.
Consv. Review, 3:18–21, 46.

1935 (with H. V. Howe) Cheniers of southwestern Louisiana. Geogr. Review, 25:449–461.

1936 Physiography of Lower Mississippi River Delta. La.
Dept. Consv., Geol. Surv., Bull. 8:3–199.

1938 Physiography of Iberville and Ascension Parishes.
La. Dept. Consv., Geol. Surv., Bull. 13:3–86.

1939 Morphologie des Mississippideltas. Geogr. Zeitsch.,
45:282–293.

1940 Quaternary history of Louisiana. Geol. Soc. Am.,
Bull. 51:1199–1234.

1942 Geomorphology of the Rhône Delta. Assoc. Am.
Geogrs., Annals, 32:149–254.

1958 Geological geomorphology. Geol. Soc. Am., Bull
69:1–22.

1964a Techniques of eustasy studies. Zeitsch. f. Geomorphol., vol. 8, Sonderhft., 8:25–42.

1946b Mass-movements in contrasting latitudes, VI Internat. Cong., INQUA (Warsaw), 4:143–153.

Smith, E. A.

1894 (with L. C. Johnson and D. W. Langdon, Jr.) Report on the coastal plain of Alabama. Ala. Geol.
Surv., Spec. Rept. 6, 759 pp.

van Lopik, J. R. (see Morgan, 1953, and Kolb).

2 / STREAM PATTERNS

Three varieties of river channels are recognized by most alluvial morphologists (Russell, 1958). The *fixed channel* is erosional in origin and ordinarily remains in essentially the same location as its bed is slowly deepened. The *braided channel* exhibits maximum complexity because it is characterized by division into numerous minor branches around lenticular bars or islands, together with the confluence of branches at various places downstream. The *meandering channel* typically is simple but winding, changing its location systematically. The discussion to follow will be concerned with channels on flood plains and will refer to examples of all three varieties. Stream patterns on flood plains, as they appear on maps or when viewed from the air, result from fluvial processes that are also responsible for creating alluvial landforms.

At the onset, it should be stated that the two most significant parts of a flood plain are the natural levees along channels, and the basins between them. Natural levees may have widths from a few tens of feet along smaller streams up to several miles along rivers the size of the Lower Mississippi (Pl. 5). Their crests attain levels established by overflow during floods and their back-slopes are ordinarily concave skyward and vary in steepness from as much as a drop of ten feet in a few hundred

PLATE 5. New Orleans occupies the natural levee of the Mississippi River and its backslope leading to Lake Ponchartrain (foreground). Downstream land nearer the levee crest is cleared and more densely populated than low basins on either side. Photograph by Davis Photographic Service.

along small but torrential streams to as little as ten feet
or less in the first mile away from the channel of a main
river. All natural levee slopes decrease gradually toward
the flatness characteristic of an adjacent basin floor.

The flow of water above a channel bed and below air
cannot exceed a rate of about fifty miles per hour. Water
started down a long, smooth incline would accelerate
and exceed that limiting velocity were its flow not slowed
by effects of frictional shear stresses of various kinds.
These stresses arise from contact with the air and the
channel bed, but those of greatest significance develop
internally, within the water itself. One example of in-
ternal shear arises because water at depth tends to follow
the course of a channel more faithfully than water close
to the surface (Vogel and Thompson, 1933). The lateral
sliding of threads of flow across those lower in the channel is but one of many examples of stress arising within
masses of flowing water.

Several kinds of flow occur in nature (Hjulström,
1935). In *laminar*, or streamline, flow, all water particles
follow parallel paths and no mixing occurs between layers at various depths. Water has to be almost stationary
in a river channel to exhibit this kind of flow, except in
a thin layer in immediate contact with the bed. Other-
wise, channel flow is *turbulent* or sinuous. In addition
to primary downchannel movement, complex secondary
motions are present that create unsteady, non-uniform
flow. To develop these motions energy is required. It is
subtracted from that available for maintaining velocity.

In turbulent flow, water develops directional and velocity pulsations; eddies, with more or less perpendicular
axes; rollers, with more or less horizontal axes; transverse
oscillations; vortices that may be visible or that appear
as non-rotating boils at the surface; bottom-scouring

swirls (Matthes, 1947); and other complex motions (Sundborg, 1956). Mixing occurs throughout flowing water. There are two types of rapid flow, *streaming* and *shooting*. At lower velocities, streaming occurs, but on slopes such as from twenty-two to twenty-six feet vertically per mile, the velocity is such that the threshold of shooting flow may be reached. The change is accompanied by a decrease in the cross section of a flowing stream that lowers and smooths the water surface. On a change back to streaming, hydraulic jump occurs, and the water surface is promptly raised and roughened. Practically all flow along floodplain channels is streaming, but locally increased gradients may develop shooting. The critical velocity at which the change occurs is influenced by bed roughness, a factor that influences turbulence and streaming, rather than shooting flow.

The *erosion*, or entrainment, of a sedimentary particle from the wetted perimeter of a channel depends on a random grouping of factors and hence presents a problem of a statistical nature. In general, the size of particles, their density, shape, degree of sorting, and tendencies to be cohesive may be regarded as passive factors. When these are overcome by active factors associated with the flow of water, sediment particles become entrained (Rubey, 1938). Although it is customary to relate entrainment to *critical erosion velocities*, the process is far more complex than the relation implies. In general, as Hjulström, Sundborg, and others have pointed out, in homogeneous sediments on flat beds, the particle entrained at minimum erosion velocity has a diameter approximating that of coarsest silt or finest sand. On a large river with a velocity slightly less than one-half mile per hour, extremely light particles, such as fine-sand-sized pieces of lignite, will be entrained. To detach grains as heavy as fine quartz sand from the bottom the velocity would have to approach one mile per hour, while for similar sized but much denser magnetite, the required

velocity would be about 10 percent higher. These velocities apply to water one meter above the channel bed.
Surface velocities in a deep channel would be considerably higher and those near the bed somewhat lower.

The entrainment of materials either finer than coarse
silt or grains coarser than fine sand requires higher velocities. Clay is ordinarily cohesive, while coarse sand or
gravel-sized sediments are heavy. All values given above
apply to flat beds, but in nature channel floors may be
irregular, so other factors enter the problem. Grains
lodged on downchannel slopes require far less velocity
for entrainment. If the slope amounts to 20° the reduction may be as much as 90 percent. As Mackin (1948)
has pointed out, this effect renders it much easier to
erode materials from channel sides than from floors and
this may be a reason why many channels in alluvium
have relatively flat floors but steep sides.

The packing of sediment also affects entrainment velocities. In loosely packed sand the porosity averages
about 40 percent and the interstices between grains are
wide enough to permit turbulent water to penetrate the
sediment and remove particles with relative ease. While
clay may have a porosity varying between 30 and 90 percent, the voids between individual particles are so small
that sediment is bound together by cohesion that renders
entrainment difficult. Nearly a centutry ago Colonel
James B. Eads, who gained fame for building a permanent bridge across the Mississippi at St. Louis, who built
successful jetties at South Pass, one of the mouths of the
Mississippi River, and who walked many miles of river
bed under a diving bell, observed that the bed and walls
of the channel below New Orleans might as well consist
of marble as of clay from the standpoint of the ability
of the river to erode them.

Lack of uniformity in sizes of bed and bank sediments
favors entrainment, but much research will be necessary
before the effects are formulated in quantitative terms.

On a flat bed consisting of loose sediment with particles
between 0.2 and 0.5 mm in diameter minimum velocity is
necessary for entrainment in comparison with that necessary for other sizes. But if particles of this range of sizes
are mixed with coarser grains the entrainment velocity
is decreased and the first grains to move are likely to
have diameters somewhat more than 0.5 mm (0.02 inch).
Once in motion, these particles travel faster and farther.

It is characteristic of alluvial deposits that they contain relatively few particles with diameters ranging from
about 1 to 6 mm (0.24 inch). There has been much spec-
ulation about this because the weathering and disin-
tegration of rocks must produce them. Apparently these
coarse sands and fine gravels are hardly allowed to rest
in water flowing sufficiently fast to entrain them. It appears probable that once entrained the particles bounce,
slide, roll, and at times rise into the suspended load until
they have completely outdistanced both coarser and finer
sediments. Although many experts have contended that
coarse sands and gravels do not accumulate on beaches
and some have postulated that they cross shelves
to lodge on continental slopes, my research during
1967 has concentrated on this problem and I have
found that these coarse sediments, in fact, occur in
unexpected abundance on the Outer Banks, North
Carolina.

If large gravels are scattered along a channel floor,
finer surrounding sediments commonly are eroded away,
leaving blocks or slabs of coarser size to accumulate res-
idually, in some cases to form a pavement on the bed.
Like the lag gravels of arid environments, a channel
pavement interferes seriously with subsequent erosion,
and water above it may be perfectly clear even in rapid
flow. A person wading in a shallow stream with rapid
flow commonly encounters pavements, particularly in
mountainous regions. The weight of his body concentrated in an area the size of his foot may press through

a thin shield of gravel, allowing rapid entrainment of underlying fine sediment which rises as plumes and increases turbidity in his vicinity.

Once entrained, sediment moves in various ways along channels (Gilbert, 1914). In the immediate proximity of the bed a *contact load* advances mainly by particles sliding or rolling downcurrent. Above this is a *saltation load* in intermittent transport (McGee, 1908). Some particles rotate and experience hydrodynamic lift, while others bounce along, like a ball tossed down a long hallway. Higher in the channel is the *suspended load,* kept up either by buoyancy or, most importantly, by upward components of turbulence. Although turbulence distributes water particles in all directions and the total upward movement balances that downward, in the case of entrained sedimentary load the source of material is the channel bed and the main transportational effect of turbulence is upward transfer, prolonging the length of the journey of each particle downstream, as it moves with the general flow.

Transportation velocity is an approximate value expressing an estimate of the minimum current speed required to keep sediment of a given size in suspension. Commonly it is regarded as amounting to about two-thirds of the velocity necessary for entrainment for sediment coarser than silt (Sundborg, 1956). In both velocity concepts the degree of turbulence present in flowing water is actually more significant than the speed of its downchannel movement, but the intensity of turbulence is inadequately measurable, whereas current meters have been measuring flow velocities for many years. In general, it is believed that turbulence increases at a rate that somewhat exceeds the square of the current velocity. The velocity and amount of turbulence necessary to keep a mineral grain or fragment of rock in suspension increases as particles are larger and heavier. Working relentlessly against all factors tending to keep load above a channel bed is the force of gravity. All particles settle at appropriate *sedimentation rates* according to their size, shape, and weight.

As a practical matter the load of a stream is divided into two parts, with an indefinite transition zone between. Contact, saltation, and other loads close to the bottom are called *bed load*, while in the water above the load is regarded as *suspended*. With increased velocities the turbulence increases and the distribution of particles of various sizes becomes more uniform through the water depth (Hjulström, 1935). Coarser materials are tossed up into parts of the flow where, with less velocity, only fine grains would be present. The surface of a stream becomes most turbid during times of flood.

The suspended load may be sampled and estimated with considerable precision, but evaluations of bed load are highly imprecise, both for the reason that its upper boundary is poorly defined and because only inadequate sampling methods have been devised. Estimates ordinarily vary between 2 and 60 percent of total load, and it is supposed that on the average about 20 percent of transported sediment moves as bed load. But I have observed a case where practically all transportation occurs as bed load. Near the mouth of the Sakarya River on the Black Sea coast of western Anatolia, I looked through exceptionally clear water to see coarse sand grains rolling and bouncing on a bed of similar material.

DEPOSITIONAL PROCESSES

The sedimentation rate is the velocity with which particles settle in still water. For a particle of coarse clay, the rate may be eight inches per day, but for coarse sand it amounts to about twelve feet per minute. A particle in transport is propelled ahead by current velocity, kept off the bottom by processes such as hydrodynamic lift and turbulence, but must, at length, settle under the influence of gravity. Thus it becomes *deposited*. Many

particles settle into the moving bed load, from whence
they may be returned into suspension, but others settle
more permanently on the channel floor or on land surfaces beyond channel boundaries. When floods cause
water to overflow natural levee crests, most of the sediment carried away from the channel is suspended load
and therefore is relatively fine in comparison with the
bed load that moves ahead along the channel floor. For
that reason, while the natural levees of the Mississippi
in Louisiana are composed mainly of silt or fine sand,
the channel bed is relatively coarse and remains sandy
almost to the river mouths (passes), about 100 miles
below New Orleans.

While, in general, the sediments in the channel or that
have been deposited on the flood plain become finer
downstream in the Lower Mississippi Valley, this longi-
tudinal *sorting* is far more gradual than that transverse
to the channel. On the crests of natural levees, we find
a concentration of coarser parts of the suspended load,
deposited because turbulence decreases promptly as
overflow velocity is sharply reduced below channel velocity. The sorting toward the floor of the adjacent basin
is effective because overflow normally occurs in relatively
thin sheets that spread out and diminish in velocity, so
that only sediment of finer and finer size remains suspended. In the backswamps beyond levees, little remains
other than finest clay or colloidal particles. Typically,
the result is a deposit of coarse silt or sand on the levee
crest, grading basinward into fine silt, clay, and eventually ooze, a sorting that may be observed within distances
of a mile, or very rarely in more than ten miles.

In the passes of the Lower Mississippi River, channel
beds rise toward seaward bars at a rate of from three to
five feet per mile for a distance of twenty miles. This
slope hinders low-stage sediment transport to a degree
that causes large dunelike and forward-creeping sand
waves to form and floor the channel. Shallowness of

channel-mouth bars permits thick sludge to accumulate in the lower parts of passes during the prolonged periods of low water. The sludge is colloidal and becomes so dense that bar pilots fear that a ship entering the river will be slowed down to the point of losing steerageway before reaching better water. Both sand waves and sludge are normally flushed away during the rising river stages of early winter or spring. The sand beyond the confines of channels is transported by longshore currents to spits and beaches that form along coasts west of the passes. The colloids, clay, finest silt, and other easily moved objects move seaward where they settle and accumulate as *prodelta clay* or continue their transport across the shelf.

DELTAIC STREAM PATTERNS

The channel patterns of a delta stream are determined by subaqueous processes. In plan they superficially resemble subaerial braided, or anastomotic, floodplain

PLATE 6. Deltaic stream patterns below Pass a Loutre Crevasse of 1891, where most of Garden Island Bay has either become land or very shoal water since that date. Trees grow densely on natural levees and bars. Photograph by J. P. Morgan.

channels (Pl. 6) (Russell, 1954). The effects of underwater origin may be seen on most deltas or in alluviating
estuaries. Lenticular bars or islands appear in channels,
dividing their flow. This process may be repeated numerous times so that rivers are divided into many diverging
and converging branches.

When an alluviating river reaches the sea or a large
lake, its natural levees by no means terminate along the
shore. They continue outward as submarine features,
with crests along the sides of bands of more rapidly
seaward-flowing river water. Lacking the bank confine-
ment typical upstream, currents of river water tend to
flare and attain greater width on extending out into a
lake or the sea, but the hydraulic principles that obtain
upstream only gradually are replaced by those characteristic of the larger body of water. Upstream, separate
threads of most intense turbulent exchange of water and
sediment particles normally occur somewhat below mid-
channel depth, toward channel sides (Leighly, 1932).
In these locations, shear stress imposed on water by friction caused by flow over the bed is reinforced by friction
from channel walls. This effect continues seaward or
lakeward. The more intense threads of turbulent exchange toward each channel side result locally in more
effective forward transport of load, between which the
water is somewhat more slack, exchange is less pronounced, and deposition is favored (Fig. 13). A delta
stream with flaring natural levees thus tends to develop
at least one mid-channel shoal. These are likely to become
bars and eventually islands between permanent channels. Separated channels also tend to flare seaward, develop natural levees of their own, and form the next gen-
eration of mid-channel bars. The number of individual
channels therefore tends to increase seaward in geomet-
rical progression. That full development of the progression is not realized as a rule depends on the erosional activities of waves and swells. A zone of conflict develops

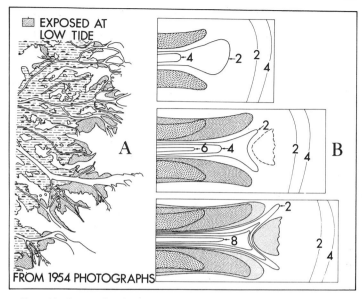

Fig. 13. Seaward advance of natural levees and development of branching channels (after Welder). In A, the dotted areas are covered at high tide. Channel depths in B are typical of the Mississippi Delta if expressed in feet.

along a delta front between the tendency of river levees and bars to advance seaward as submarine features and the power of the sea to straighten outlines of coasts composed of unconsolidated sedimentary deposits. Some deltas are wave-dominated and exhibit relatively smooth shorelines but others that are better nourished by supplies of sediment or that are located in more tranquil seas push their complicated fronts seaward more successfully, in some cases for many tens of miles.

The natural levees of a flood plain continue into a delta as bifurcating subaerial landforms, then advance seaward as submarine features. As a delta distributary advances its submarine natural levees gain in volume and their crests eventually become narrow strips of land. Areas over which fish swim become flats upon which birds stand in water that may barely immerse their talons, after which a plant succession gains foothold,

involving grass, willows, and eventually other trees characteristic of dry land, among which hackberry, prickly
ash, and oak are numerous in coastal Louisiana. It is in
this way that stream patterns are established in deltas
and natural levees grow seaward to separate basins open
toward the coast. The point should be stressed that all
major channel patterns in a delta are essentially those
originally established under water (Welder, 1955). Later
on, some distributaries are closed off at points of branching by extensions of natural levees along more favored
channels. The beheaded channels, when robbed both of
current and sedimentary load, are likely to persist for
a long time. In the Lower Delta of the Mississippi these
are called "blind passes," and commonly bear names
such as Fool's Bayou; traps for the ignorant who enter
from the gulf expecting to find a route into the main river.

Deltaic stream patterns may develop within a few
years in bays that suddenly become subject to alluviation because a crevasse channel has been established
across the natural levee of some active channel. An excellent example in the Lower Delta is Garden Island Bay
which first received crevasse flow in 1891 (Fig. 4).
The bay was up to nine feet deep before the crevasse
occurred but is practically filled today, even though
maps show land covering little more than half of its area.
The part remaining submerged is extremely shallow and
continues underwater the channel complexity of the part
that has become land. All channels are shoal and the
basins between them have been alluviated almost to sea
level. I have spent many hours dragging shallow-draft
skiffs across the area in search of channels deep enough
to float them.

The submarine natural levees off of Main Pass, the
major northward distributary of the Lower Delta, advance so rapidly and shift positions so widely over a belt
about three miles wide that pilots with long experience
are likely to run aground when attempting to navigate
channels they may have used a few weeks previously.

Even more astonishing is the condition off the shore of
the Sakarya River, about ninety miles east of Istanbul,
on the Black Sea. The submarine channels shift about
so freely that a pilot spends most of every day keeping
track of changes so that he can guide boats into the river
channel late in the afternoon. Some of these left for the
Black Sea only eight or ten hours previously.

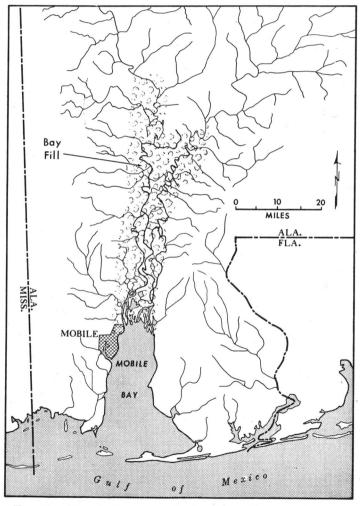

Fig. 14. Although the estuary of a few thousand years ago appears
only about three-quarters filled on maps, Mobile Bay is actually very
shoal over broad areas.

Many of the finest examples of deltaic stream patterns occur in alluviating estuaries. Mobile Bay, on the coast of Alabama, is an excellent specimen. Some 3,000 years ago, when sea level reached its present stand, a long estuary developed (Fig. 14), into which several large rivers converged. The river-borne sediment collected rapidly, established typical deltaic patterns, and by now has nearly filled the original estuary. As in the case of Garden Island Bay, areas shown as water on charts are mainly shoal. Many small meandering channels lead from river channels into basins within the alluviated land area.

The valley of the Amazon is even more spectacular. It extended across Brazil as a narrow and undoubtedly scenic estuary when sea level was approaching its present stand (Russell, 1958). The river, heavily laden with sediment, deposited alluvium enough to build an elongate delta that at present extends nearly to the coast. The pattern of river bifurcation, the presence of numer-

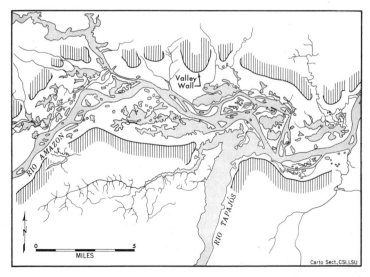

Fig. 15. Deltaic channels of the lower Amazon in the vicinity of Santarém, about 450 miles west of Belém. The many branches around lenticular islands are typical of stream patterns created under water.

ous lenticular islands, the occurrence of deep holes at various places along the bed of the main and branch channels, as well as the systems of natural levees and basins between valley walls, are all those of submarine origin (Fig. 15). Here, as in Mobile Bay, after the deposits accumulated high enough above the original estuarine floor to exhibit dry-land features, natural levees separated basins, as they do in normal flood plains, and overflow streams developed vigorously meandering channels leading across levee crests or at least down their backslopes into the basins (Sternberg, 1959a). As the volume of sediment contributed by the Amazon was much greater than that coming down its tributaries below Manaus, bars and downstream continuations of the levees have partially dammed old tributary branches of the estuary system, forming many lakes that narrow upstream in funnel fashion. Connecting outflow channels cross bars along the alluvial barriers with widths and depths appropriate for their discharges.

GREAT MEANDER AND MISSISSIPPI FLOOD PLAINS

Gerard H. Matthes, twin brother of the eminent geologist François and in my opinion an outstanding hydrologist and foremost alluvial morphologist, described the Lower Mississippi River as *poised* (Matthes, 1941). Both aggradation and degradation occur on its flood plain and both scour and fill along its channel, but over periods of time such as the last ten centuries there has been little change in valley slope. The hallmark of a poised river is its meandering course.

My studies of meandering took me to the river that supplied us with the technical term, the Great Meander of southwestern Anatolia (Russell, 1954). The main reason for the investigation was to ascertain whether the river actually meanders and if so what kind of meanders it displays. Any person who has visited a number of geological "type localities," the places where particular rock units or other geologic phenomena were first described, finds that pioneer investigators were attracted in most cases to odd sites, commonly affected by unrecognized land slips or other unusual features. He gradually develops a stoical attitude, particularly after learning that much more meaningful exposures exist elsewhere. It was an agreeable experience to find that, indeed, the Great Meander is an excellent type locality, not only for meandering but also for many other processes involved in floodplain development.

For more than eighty miles the Meander follows an east-west graben, a down-dropped fault block that determines the position of a practically straight valley. For the first forty miles downstream from the town of Saraköy, alluvial deposits of rivers from the north push the river against the southern wall of the graben (Pl. 7), much as rivers leading from the Sierra Nevada have formed alluvial cones that crowd the San Joaquin toward the western side of the Great Valley of California. There is little or no meandering along this part of the Meander's course. Above Aydin, however, the river begins to meander in characteristic fashion on a widening flood plain of its own creation. This channel pattern is interrupted at places by deposits of rivers from the south, particularly those of the Ak and Çine. Both of these, and some other tributaries, are what the French term "hydrologic monsters," with little flow during seasons of dryness but during rainy periods fantastic floods appear capable of transporting boulders up to several feet in diameter (Pl. 8). The Meander, where overwhelmed by transported load, assumes a braided pattern for several miles downstream from tributary junctions after which it returns to more orderly meandering. Many now-abandoned courses of the river characterize its flood plain as do cut-off lakes in relict meander loops (Pl. 9). Below Söke, the river again is influenced by fault control (Fig. 16). A compar-

PLATE 7. (*Above*)
Straight course of the Great
Meander along its south valley wall is a result of rapid
growth of alluvial cones on
tributaries from the north.

PLATE 8. (*Left*) Gravel
bar of the Durance near its
confluence with the Rhône,
southern France.

PLATE 9. (*Below*) Aban-
doned loop on the channel of
the Great Meander River between Incirliova and Koçarli,
Turkey.

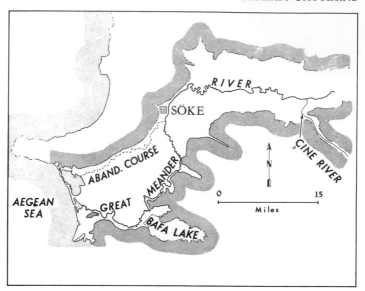

Fig. 16. The Great Meander was diverted from its old course west of Söke to swing across its valley. Miletus was located on the south valley wall near the "G" of "Great."

atively straight course dating possibly from more than 2,000 years ago followed the north side of a graben directly to the sea, but more recent courses have crossed to the south side of the valley and have deposited so much alluvium that since the time of Herodotus the Meander Delta has advanced over ten miles, building its natural levees so that they dammed an arm of its estuary, creating Bafa Lake, and ending the history of nearby Miletus as a seaport.

The Lower Mississippi River exemplifies many features characteristic of the Meander. Downstream from Thebes Gap in southern Illinois, more than one-fifth of the course of the Mississippi is braided (Friedkin, 1945). This occurs along reaches and is best developed where bed and bank materials consist of coarse sand or gravel, so is more typical up- than down-valley. Braided parts of the river exhibit many lenticular islands, locally called *towheads*, and actively shifting channels. The width of the river exceeds that downstream and varies tremendously with river stage. Between Cairo and Memphis, the average width across reaches amounts to 3,041 feet at lowest stage and 7,034 feet during flood. In comparison, between Baton Rouge and New Orleans, where the bed is deeper and consists of finer sand and the banks are of silt bound by clay, the contrast is between 2,381 and 2,907 feet. At low stage, the Louisiana reaches are about 78 percent as wide as those above Memphis, but at high stage several reaches above Memphis are nearly two and one-half times as wide. Upstream channels exhibit conspicuous braiding and shoaling. They impose enormous upkeep costs in maintaining a navigable channel twelve feet or more in depth when the river is low.

While the Mississippi does not have hydrologic-monster tributaries, such as the Ak or Çine, alluvial cones from rivers such as the Arkansas influence valley-slope gradients considerably. As conspicuously exhibited along the Po and Rhône rivers of Europe, each cone has a damming effect and decreases valley slope upstream, where meandering is favored, while on cone slopes downvalley, where velocity increases, both bed and channel-side sediments are entrained more readily, so that braiding is favored (Russell, 1942). Some tributaries locally introduce significant coarse sand or gravel loads that promote braiding tendencies. The last example downstream is Thompson Creek, about twenty-four miles above Baton Rouge. Less than four miles downstream most of the coarse sediment accumulates on Profit Island, a large towhead that provides a renewable resource for mining aggregates for concrete.

The Lower Mississippi also resembles the Meander in exhibiting structural control of its valley, as well as of many individual segments of its course (Fisk, 1941). Below Thebes Gap, where the river enters the old, broad valley of the Ohio (Fig. 11) the flood plain follows a structural trough that continues southward to coastal

Louisiana. This feature is present structurally in rocks extending back through the Tertiary into the latter part of the Mesozoic and by some is called "the Mississippi Embayment." Although the feature was once an embayment in the sense that it was in part occupied during the late Eocene by marine waters extending from the Gulf of Mexico, the term, "embayment," is misleading because throughout most of its history the shoreline has remained far to the south. More appropriate is the expression "Mississippi Structural Trough." This structural feature is not without complications. Conspicuous active fault zones cross it both in northeastward and northwestward directions. Grabens, fault lines, and other lineations parallel the fault zones and influence the course of the river today, as they have done throughout the Quaternary. Examples occur at various places where reaches are considerably longer than those typical at crossings, where the river passes from one meander bend to another. Any long, straight channel segment is suspect as having been determined by the position of some graben or single line of displacement along a fault. Where borings have been made on both sides of reaches the evidence of vertical offset ordinarily is established.

Both the Meander and Mississippi meander so freely that in many cases their loops have been accentuated to the degree necessary for forming neck cut-offs. Mark Twain referred to these cut-offs in a classic, tongue-in-cheek manner (Clemens). He noted the shortening of up to twenty miles or so at many places as some meander loop was cut off during historic time. Upon the basis of adding reduced river distances he calculated that Cairo and New Orleans would be only 1.75 miles apart in 742 years, and elaborated upon the satisfaction of solving problems scientifically. Of course, he knew as well as most river engineers that each developing meander loop lengthens the channel by an amount that is cancelled when a cut-off forms and that so many examples occur along the Lower Mississippi that they neutralize each other. What may be regarded as somewhat amazing is the fact that all of the twenty courses identified by Fisk as having been occupied during the last thirty centuries have practically the same length, about 1,100 miles, between Cairo and the Gulf of Mexico.

In its history of creating cut-offs and wandering about on its flood plain, the Meander resembles the Mississippi in having been subject to structural controls but has not caused itself to become sharply confined to definite *meander belts*. The Mississippi has that characteristic because it transports a heavy load of silt and clay.

When the Mississippi establishes a neck cut-off, the abandoned channel becomes a relict meander loop of size and depth appropriate to the discharge, local valley slope, and bed materials. The abandoned loop is crescentic, with horns pointed toward the river (Fig. 17). The water in the cut-off is relatively slack and tends to accumulate sediment rapidly if a supply is on hand. At each end of the loop natural-levee dams are created in a very few years, so most of the isolated loop becomes a stagnant lake. If there is some flow between the main channel and the lake at time of flood, deltas form at lake ends. These may enlarge rather rapidly for a while but the connecting channels are likely to become clogged and the rate of sediment introduction from the main channel eventually drops to little or nothing. Such sediment as reaches the lake is derived from suspended load in the main channel and hence is relatively fine in size. More persistent is the accumulation of clay in the lake resulting from a continuing supply of local plant remains that decompose into soft ooze. In time a deposit of silt and clay accumulates in the lake and may attain considerable thickness—over 120 feet in an extreme example, in an old cut-off lake near Lake Providence, Louisiana. These deposits are called *clay plugs* (Fisk, 1947). Where their thickness amounts to 40 feet or more they resist erosional

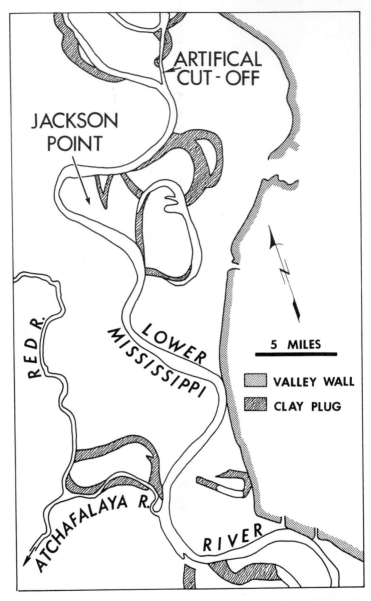

Fig. 17. Clay plugs have formed in many cut-off meander loops along the Lower Mississippi River but are not present to prevent diversion into Red River in the vicinity of Jackson Point, Louisiana (after Fisk).

activities along the channel and if present in considerable numbers confine the course of the Mississippi to a definite meander belt.

The Mississippi within a meander belt is confined in about the way that pigs are trapped when driven down a lane between fences. A pig is held by fences, the river by clay plugs along both sides of the meander belt. If a pig escapes through some hole in the fence, it is difficult to get him back into the lane. If the river escapes from its meander belt, a *diversion* is established and the new course leads downstream through basins and in some cases along channels used and abandoned at some earlier time. The continuity of clay plugs along the present meander belt of the Lower Mississippi is so complete that for some centuries diversion is improbable except in one area, near Jackson Point, where no clay plugs stand in the way of permitting diversion into Red River, thence to the gulf along the Atchafalaya River (Fig. 17). The new course would be considerably shorter and steeper than the existing channel past Baton Rouge and New Orleans. Within a few years the new course would enlarge sufficiently to accommodate the entire discharge of the river, build its own set of natural levees, and begin constructing a delta out into the Gulf of Mexico. The abandoned channel would become a relatively stagnant, saline estuary. Although the river would no longer serve as a source of water supply for New Orleans and other places below Baton Rouge, its channel would remain much in its present condition for several centuries after diversion and would be useful as a commercial waterway as long as connections with the gulf were maintained. By means of a lock and short canal, navigation could be continued into upstream parts of the river system.

During the last thirty centuries there have been only five or six major diversions of the Lower Mississippi. Most of these occurred in northern Louisiana, some 200 miles inland. Their locations, in all cases, depended on

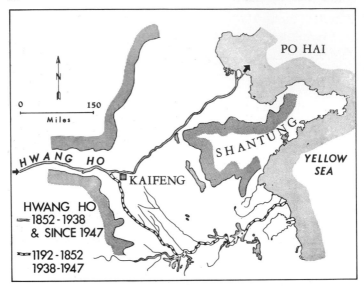

Fig. 18. Known main courses of the Hwang Ho below its diversion
point near Kaifeng, China.

the presence of faults and in no way were related to delta
growth. Thus the river history resembles that of the
Hwang Ho, of northern China, which experienced a
number of diversions into courses on one side or the other
of Shantung Peninsula (Fig. 18). The place where diversions occurred lies about 250 miles inland, near Kaifeng.
The Tarim River of central Asia has adopted courses
leading either to Lop Nor or a terminal basin some 200
miles away, according to local changes in the area where
diversions occurred. The last two major diversions were
separated by an interval of sixteen centuries (Hedin,
1940).

The efficacy of clay plugs at least forty feet deep to
hold the Mississippi within its meander belt depends
upon characteristics of the process of meandering. Generally speaking, for a concave (or cut) bank to recede, it
is necessary for local scour to deepen the channel bed
sufficiently to reduce the foundational support of prisms
of bank material so that they slump or slide off into the

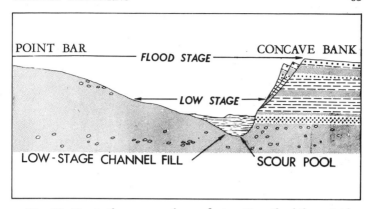

Fig. 19. Key to the process of meandering. Growth of the point bar favors deepening of a scour pool across the channel. Portions of the concave (cut) bank slide into the pool, shifting the channel away from the bar (after Fisk).

channel (Fig. 19). In places where clay plugs are present in the vicinity of scour pools, insufficient undermining occurs and the channel fails to migrate into the concave bank. If little ability exists to deepen scour pools a meander loop is not accentuated and the river remains confined to its meander belt. If the sediments on the bed of a river are coarse and that characteristic applies to the floodplain alluvium as well, as in the case of the Great Meander River, no clay plugs form and the river is free to migrate to any part of its flood plain, and does so except where locally trapped for structural or stratigraphic reasons.

ALLUVIAL MEANDERING

When viewed from the air a freely meandering river ordinarily exhibits conspicuous point bars on convex sides of bends, first on one bank, then on the other (Pl. 10). If the bars are sandy, as commonly is the case, they stand out as white areas, even where the rainfall is sufficient to establish forests, as along streams leading to the north coast of the Gulf of Mexico. Sundborg has designated the areas of bar formation as constituting the "sedimentation side" of a river (Sundborg, 1956). The conclusions of Matthes (1941) and observations of Friedkin (1945) demonstrate that sediment reaching a bar arrives mainly as bed load originating in the scour pool below the concave bank next upstream. While some bed load manages to cross the channel on reaches between bends, most of it remains on its own side of the channel. If not deposited on one bar, it is likely to come to rest on the next bar downstream on the same side of the channel.

Quite commonly helicoidal flow has been regarded as the cause of meandering. The supporting explanation regards threads of flowing water as descending to greater depths in approaching concave banks, causing scour, and as ascending toward convex bars, causing deposition. But as a result of many observations by investigators at the Waterways Experiment Station, United States Army, Corps of Engineers, it has been concluded that helicoidal flow is not a factor involved in alluvial meandering

PLATE 10. Vigorous meandering of Laramie River, Wyoming, together with channel scars left on its flood plain. Photograph by J. R. Balsey, U. S. Geological Survey.

(Vogel and Thompson, 1933; Matthes, 1941 and 1947). Observations in scale models with beds of movable sediment indicate that helicoidal flow has an insignificant effect, nor has it been detected in the Lower Mississippi. Sediment is attracted toward point bars because the intensity of turbulence decreases in that direction. Bed load moves from places where turbulence is more intense toward places where it falls off and deposition is most pronounced where the water is relatively slack.

Point bars are composed of somewhat coarser sediment than is characteristic of natural-levee crests in the vicinity. The bars are nourished mainly by bed load, whereas the levee crests are built mainly of sediment carried as suspended load. If coarse sand or gravel is present in the local bed load it works upslope and comes to rest on bars rather than elsewhere, because it is impelled by turbulent flow toward areas of lesser activity. Bars grow most rapidly either just prior to or somewhat after the passage of flood crests. As they advance into former channel positions they become essentially permanent deposits and protect from removal all earlier parts of the accumulation.

Along the Lower Mississippi, willows promptly become established on any new accretion deposit and attain a height of about three feet within a year. As they grow upward at about that rate for several years, a point bar commonly displays a terrace-like succession of trees from which the frequency of floods during recent years may be deciphered either by observing tree heights or counting their annual rings. With continuing accretion, the record of similar history is left by fairly concentric systems of low ridges and swales. Plate 11 illustrates this same topography in Sweden. Each ridge is the deposit of an individual flood. Now and then, some swale may become a branch channel across a bar at time of flood, and occasionally a channel of this kind enlarges and deepens to gain some permanency, in which case it be-

PLATE 11. Typical bar and swale topography on a point bar on the Klarälven, Sweden. The point advanced toward the low trees beyond the hay field.

comes a *chute*. Occasionally, depending mainly on flood-current directions just upstream, a chute diverts the river, shortening its course locally. These chute cut-offs are minor in effect as compared to neck cut-offs each of which may reduce river distance by ten miles or more. Most of a bar deposit will remain in position, safe from erosion, until some entirely new river course crosses it. While dissolved load, colloids, or particles of fine clay might travel from the Rocky Mountains to the Gulf of Mexico in less than a year, a grain of coarse sand wherever introduced into the river, may not be transported beyond the first point bar downstream, so its trip from Cairo to the gulf may take many thousands of years and during most of the time it will be at rest in bar deposits. Many grains, of course, become indefinitely incorporated in floodplain alluvium.

Bar alluviation explains a process of sediment integration called trading (R. J. and R. D. Russell, 1939). Each tributary of the Lower Mississippi contributes load of a distinctive character. The Ohio, Upper Mississippi, St. Francis, White, Arkansas, and Red transport quite different suites of mineral grains and rock fragments. But after reaching the flood plain of the Mississippi, these differences soon disappear because tributary loads are trapped in bars and the load picked up downstream is that of the main flood plain. Bank caving and channel

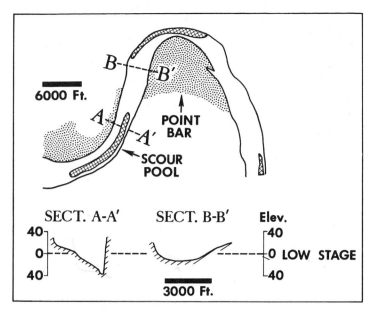

Fig. 20. Channel characteristics of bends of rivers flowing on alluvium. Flow is from left to right and the scale is typical of the Lower Mississippi (after Fisk).

scouring furnish the new load. In either case, it is derived from floodplain alluvium, ·which is a thoroughly integrated mixture of all tributary contributions.

One effect of bar growth is channel narrowing, which, in turn, forces the river to assume one or both of the alternatives of increasing its velocity or eroding its channel sufficiently to maintain its cross-sectional area (Fig. 20). Actually, both alternatives come into play if the channel is confined to alluvium. Increased velocity is accompanied by increased turbulence and scour capability. The scour pool, formed and deepened across channel from the point bar, promotes bank caving, retreat of the concave bank, and hence the process of meandering. Caved and scoured sediment is rapidly transported to the next point bar downstream, accentuating meandering there, and so on as far as bed and bank materials permit.

Estimates of transported sediment load have little meaning, except for the places where measurements are made. A river is far more turbid between a scour pool and the next bar downstream than between that bar and the following scour pool. Transported load always has an important component of motion toward places where turbulence is less intense. Slack water becomes an excellent sediment trap and the relatively slack water on the bar side is favored as a site for deposition in comparison with the water on the scour-pool side of a channel. This, of course, favors asymmetry of channel cross-sections on all bends. The slope from the bar is relatively gentle toward the deepest part of the bed, which lies not far from the cut-bank.

During the crest of an extreme flood, the process of meandering is less effective than during the latter part of the preceding rising stage or the early stages of the subsequent falling of the river. The reason for this is that during flood crests the slope of the water surface, *hydraulic gradient*, approaches closest approximation to floodplain slope, *valley gradient*. If the Lower Mississippi could be held at extreme flood stage for some years, its meanders would disappear because during the crest of a flood the thread of maximum current velocity straightens appreciably. It moves toward point bars and tends to erode them (Matthes, 1941). The pilot of a river boat will take advantage of this in traveling upstream. He will hug cut banks during flood, whereas at all other times, he will stay as close as feasible to points.

<hr>

EFFECTS OF STAGE VARIATION

<hr>

While it is commonly believed that increasing stage favors erosion of channels and falling stage is accompanied by deposition, a far better generalization would regard highest stage as a time of maximum change, both of erosion and deposition, and low stage a time when practically nothing happens in creating changes in channel morphology. When erosion is at its peak, deposition is also most vigorous along rivers bedded in alluvium.

In the case of meandering rivers, the vigor of pool scour, bank caving, and bar deposition reach maximum intensity when the stage and velocity are high. During the peak of an extraordinary flood, erosional vigor may outstrip depositional activities along various segments of a channel and changes in stream patterns establish trends toward developing straighter courses. During rising stage, however, pools are scoured and bar growth is rapid. The first sediment entrained by pool scour accumulated toward the end of the last falling stage is picked up readily. Newly wetted parts of the bank are comparatively stable, however, and the contribution from caving is smaller than at an equivalent stage when river stage is falling. Banks saturated for some days or weeks are particularly susceptible to caving and the engineers responsible for flood control are hopeful that any fall in stage will be orderly and gradual so that bank subsidence, is minimized. After stage is considerably lowered, the scour pools begin to fill, bed load ceases to move in appreciable quantities, and bar-building terminates. If low stage is prolonged practically all bank caving stops and the volume of suspended load decreases to a degree where the river becomes relatively clear.

Under natural conditions, flood-overtopping of natural levees occurs when bank-full stage is reached. Most crevasses occur across concave-bank levees, where they divert sediment in suspension, rather than bed load (Fig. 21). The amount diverted is a relatively small fraction of the total load. If bank-full stage lasts for a considerable time, crevasse channels may become fairly deep and divert a portion of each high-stage flow for several years or decades, in which case they become more or less permanent distributaries. Sooner or later, however, meandering ordinarily causes course modifications that change the direction of the thread of maximum current

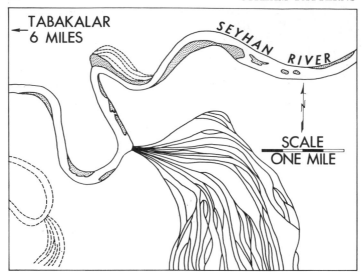

Fig. 21. Channels below a crevasse on the lower Seyhan River, Tur-key, are associated with complex microtopography of their own depo-sition. The river flows toward the left and is heavily loaded with sand, some of which has been deposited in recent years as exceptionally large bars.

velocity and the distributary is sealed off by natural-levee deposition.

Only small parts of the Lower Mississippi now display natural conditions, except along segments where the river impinges against high valley walls. Artificial levees supplement natural-levee crests in protecting adjacent basins from flooding. That is the only purpose of an arti-ficial levee; it does nothing to prevent channel migra-tion, because the critical point of erosional attack lies deep in the channel. An artificial levee on a concave bank is normally replaced by one farther basinward as a bend is accentuated. The "ultimate set-back" along the Lower Mississippi will be located according to the pat-tern of clay plugs in the vicinity. Each is a bastion that forms a nodal point in plans for flood control (Fisk, 1947).

Revetments, such as walls of solid concrete, mats of concrete blocks, or fascine willow mattresses, slow down but can never completely control bend development.

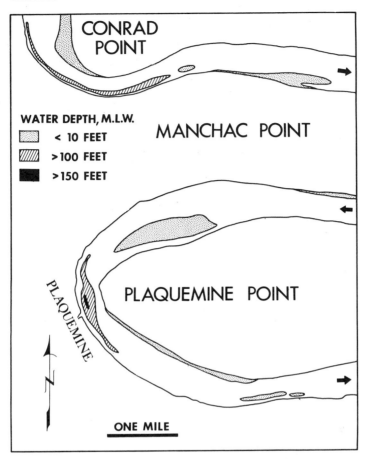

CONRAD
POINT

WATER DEPTH, M.L.W.

▢ < 10 FEET

▨ >100 FEET

■ >150 FEET

MANCHAC POINT

PLAQUEMINE POINT

PLAQUEMINE

N

ONE MILE

Fig. 22. The advance of Plaquemine Point, south of Baton Rouge, Louisiana, accounts for an exceptionally deep scour pool that renders the site of the town of Plaquemine highly precarious.

Scour pools deepen below them as the relentless and generally intractable process of bar building occurs on the opposite point, and the revetment eventually slides into the river. Where heroic measures are taken in which massive concrete revetments are built, as in the attempt to preserve the location af the town of Plaquemine, a few miles below Baton Rouge, the result has been that of creating extraordinarily deep scour pools. The pool near Plaquemine is over 150 feet deep (Fig. 22). A revetment above it perches uncertainly. Paving an entire channel, from one bank to the other, however, has the effect of placing the river in an artificial flume, where it may stay quite permanently. A successful example protects the Huey P. Long Bridge west of New Orleans.

The fate of the abandoned channel below a point of diversion or the rate of filling of a cut-off lake depends primarily on the distribution of turbulence intensity along the main river in its vicinity. If bed load travels freely toward the slack water of the abandoned channel, it will soon form a barrier that dams off the channel, leaving it for some centuries with about the dimensions it had at the time of diversion. On the other hand, if the supply of bed load is smaller, the abandoned channel may retain gradually diminishing flow for some decades or centuries and slowly become clogged by alluvium. In deciphering the history of channel changes along the Lower Mississippi, or other large alluvial rivers, one considers natural levee patterns and spacing, not channel width, to decipher channel history or correlate a channel segment with some upstream equivalent (Russell, 1939b). The bends along a channel with higher discharge will be more widely spaced and the loops of meanders will be long in comparison to the meanders along streams with lesser discharge. I have found that average distances between bends along a channel for an airline distance of 100 miles or more provide a far better index of river discharge than conclusions based on criteria such as measuring radii of curvature.

The effects of stage variation on braided streams are similar in many ways to those along meandering rivers. Pattern changes originate during floods. At low stage, one may wonder why such long and elaborate bridges extend from Texas to Oklahoma across the complicated but relatively dry sandy bed of Red River. During a flood, one may hope that the bridges survive. It is then that

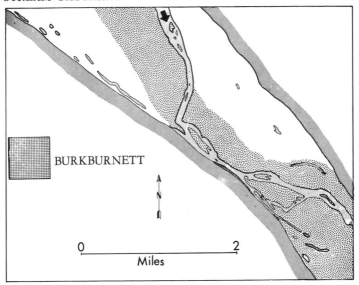

Fig. 23. Along the braided channel of Red River between Oklahoma and Texas low-stage channels are narrow and complex. During floods the channel is broad (coarse dot pattern) and comparatively simple.

intense local turbulence results in the entrainment of the greatest volumes of sand at various places along the bed and load moves rapidly toward areas of less turbulence, to be deposited not far away. As a flood subsides, both erosion and deposition decrease in intensity. At low stage, the remaining flow travels as best it can across bed irregularities created during the preceding flood. It is then that the anastomotic or braided pattern is most complicated and displayed most conspicuously (Fig. 23).

Braiding commonly occurs in sandy or gravelly alluvium, where little cohesion binds grains together. Under these conditions erosion and transport occur freely, channels become wide and shoal, and their subdivisions commonly shift about freely. But no particular grain size marks the threshold at which meandering changes into braiding. Velocity and associated turbulence commonly are conditioning factors; increases favor braided patterns. This is shown distinctly by tendencies toward meandering above, and toward braiding below, crests of alluvial cones from tributary valleys, along the Rhône, Mississippi, and other rivers. One of the great surprises experienced early in the Mississippi River Commission's program of creating numerous artificial cut-offs during the 1930's was the failure of knickpoints to develop on the channel bed. It was feared that these would migrate rapidly upstream ahead of deeply scoured pools and upset adversely pre-cutoff conditions. Instead, the increased steepness in hydraulic gradient increased turbulence, erosion, and deposition which caused the channels in cut-offs to widen and shoal so that, in many cases, they had to be dredged to maintain navigable depth.

In fixed channels, stage variability has relatively unimportant effects. While, as in all other channels, there is a tendency for a channel to adjust itself to the discharge it must carry, the changes imposed by cross-sectional enlargement toward reaching an equilibrium with flood flow, or of decreasing the section toward low-stage demands, are relatively feeble in fixed channels. In general, the channel is enlarged toward the section necessary for maximum discharge and remains much in that condition. Along an alluvial river, fixed channels ordinarily occur where the bed and banks are bound effectively by clay. In the Lower Mississippi, the channel at various points upvalley becomes fixed locally where it encounters Tertiary rocks under the floodplain alluvium. Farther downvalley for a considerable distance, it is fixed in Pleistocene clay of terrace deposits and by fault control (Fig. 22) as at places between Baton Rouge and New Orleans where sharp bends connect several closely spaced, straight reaches, each of which follows a line of weakness along a fault. Below New Orleans, the channel is fixed as it crosses Recent prodelta clay, deposited ahead of the main delta of an early channel, the Teche-Mississippi. That river course was occupied for at least 2,000 years along the western valley wall in southern

Louisiana. Its delta grew eastward toward the position of today's delta.

In clayey silt, a channel bed is relatively flat and its sides are steep. Little tendency toward meandering occurs, as is shown by the fact that the river distance between Donaldsonville and New Orleans has changed less than one-quarter mile since the date of earliest reliable surveys, because the channel is fixed in Pleistocene clay. Here is the answer to the question raised by William Morris Davis. The Mississippi is relatively straight below New Orleans for more than fifty miles between English Turn and The Forts, because it is bottomed in Recent prodelta clay, which fixes its course. At The Forts, its bed encounters coarser shoreline sediments and the channel starts meandering, but within ten miles meandering is succeeded by a true deltaic channel pattern of submarine origin (Fig. 4).

DEFORMITIES

Every irregularity in channel pattern along the Lower Mississippi can be explained, and most of them are thoroughly understood. A little drilling would clear up any others. The character of bed materials determines gross changes, but *deformities* (Matthes, 1941), or interruptions in the orderly development of meander loops, result from localized causes. A deep clay plug, for example, inhibits erosion and hence the development of loops.

A common example of deformity was described by Sten DeGeer (1906) and later meticulously examined by Sundborg (1956) along the Klarälven, the southernmost large river in Sweden. For more than fifty miles, the Klarälven follows an essentially straight valley between walls that are ordinarily less than a mile apart (Fig. 24). The river itself is an excellent example of what American physiographers called an "under-fit" stream. This terminology arose because the distance between

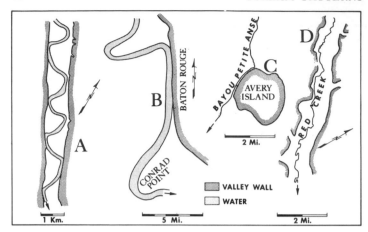

Fig. 24. Deformities: (A) thwarted meandering, Klarälven, Sweden; (B) Baton Rouge Reach, Lower Mississippi; (C) deflection around a rising salt dome, Avery Island, Louisiana; (D)entrapment along a fault zone, Stone County, southern Mississippi.

valley walls bounding a flat flood plain, regarded as corrasional in origin, may be many times wider than today's river channel. As a matter of fact, most floodplain alluvium is thick and has accumulated during the last major rise of sea level, so the distance between valley walls

PLATE 12. Meander loops of the Klarälven demanded by the discharge are too large to be accommodated between its valley walls, where bends terminate abruptly and a reach develops as a deformity.

became wider as the level of filling rose higher. Actually, the Klarälven could be regarded as "overfit" because its discharge calls for much wider meander loops than can be accommodated between its valley walls. At distances such as between one and five miles, the Klarälven initiates a meander loop, but the bend directs it toward the opposite valley wall (Pl. 12). Below most points of impingement, the downvalley course becomes straight. Ordinarily, the river hugs the wall for some distance, until a bend is initiated toward the opposite valley wall.

Fig. 25. Development of False River, the longest cut-off on the Lower Mississippi River (after Sternberg).

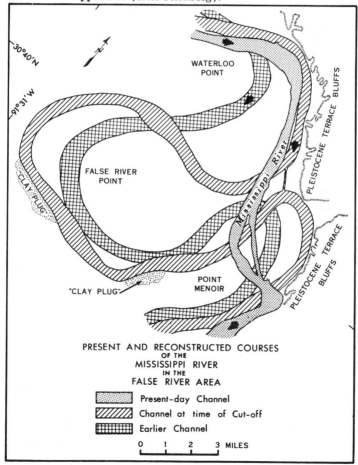

80   STREAM PATTERNS

The whole pattern is that of thwarted meandering for the reason that the width of the flood plain is not sufficient to permit full development of appropriate loops. An exactly analogous case is exhibited by the Lower Mississippi at Baton Rouge, which after many miles of free meandering, impinges against a high valley wall that interferes with loop development and is responsible for a straight course seven miles in length. This straight channel is called the Baton Rouge Reach. Downstream, the river starts meandering as it swings around Conrad Point, but soon gets trapped in clay and along faults.

Impingement of the channel against a clay plug or a concealed outcrop of a Tertiary formation produces the same type of deformity, that is, the creation of a reach downstream. One of the most striking deformities on the Lower Mississippi is False River, the last downstream and largest cut-off along the river. This was described by Sternberg (1956). Bends, both upstream and downstream, cut into the valley wall, where they became fixed (Fig. 25). Instead of orderly development, the meander loop with these fixed ends kept enlarging until it attained a length of about twenty-five miles before being deprived of flow by a neck cut-off.

Another very common kind of deformity is associated with faulting. The channel straightens out along a graben or some other line of weakened resistance to erosion (Sternberg and Russell, 1959b). Other deformities are introduced by positive behavior of the crust, as above a rising salt dome, or by the growth of alluvial cones below tributary valleys. In both cases, the river course tends to be pushed aside and inhibited from following some normal trend.

REFERENCES

Clemens, S. L. (Mark Twain) Life on the Mississippi.
DeGeer, S.
1906 Om Klarälven och dess dalgang. Ymer, 26:383–414.

Fisk, H. N.
1944 Geological investigation of the alluvial valley of the Lower Mississippi River. U. S. Army, Corps of Engineers, Mississippi River Commission (Vicksburg), 78 pp. + 33 pl.
1947 Fine-grained alluvial deposits and their effects on Mississippi River activity. U. S. Army, Corps of Engineers, Mississippi River Commission (Vicksburg), Waterways Exp. Sta., 2 vols, 82 pp + 74 pl.
Friedkin, J. F.
1945 A laboratory study of the meandering of alluvial rivers. U. S. Army, Corps of Engineers, Mississippi River Commission (Vicksburg), Waterways Exp. Sta., 40 pp. + 61 pl.
Gilbert, G. K.
1914 The transportation of debris by running water. U. S. Geol. Surv., Prof. paper 86:263 p.
Hedin, S.
1940 The wandering lake. New York (E. P. Dutton and Co.), 291 pp.
Hjulström, F.
1935 Studies of the morphological activity of rivers as illustrated by the River Fyris. Geol. Inst. Uppsala, 25:221–527. Also as a dissertation, Uppsala (Almquist and Wiksells); and in part as Transportation of detritus by moving water, in Recent Marine Sediments (P. D. Trask, ed.), Tulsa (Am. Assoc. Petrol. Geols.), 1939, p. 5–47; reprinted, 1955, by Soc. Econ. Paleontols. and Mineralogs (Tulsa).
Leighly, J. B.
1932 Toward a theory of the morphological significance of turbulence in the flow of water in streams. Univ. Calif. Publ. Geogr., 6:1–22.
McGee, W J
1908 Outlines of hydrology. Geol. Soc. Am., Bull. 19: 193–200.
Mackin, J. H.
1948 Concept of the graded river. Geol. Soc. Am., Bull. 59:463–512.
Matthes, G. H.
1941 Basic aspects of stream-meandering. Am. Geophys. U., Trans. 1941:632–636.
1947 Macroturbulence in natural stream flow. Am. Geo-

phys. U., Trans. 28:255–265.

Rubey, W. W.
1938 The force required to move particles on a stream bed. U. S. Geol. Surv., Prof. Paper 186:121–141.

Russell, R. D. (see R. J. Russell, 1939a)

Russell, R. J. (see Sternberg, 1959b)
1939a (with R. D. Russell) Mississippi River Delta sedimentation, in Recent Marine Sediments (see reference, above, F. Hjulström), p. 153–177.
1939b Louisiana stream patterns, Am. Assoc. Petrol. Geols., Bull. 23:1199–1277.
1942 Geomorphology of the Rhône Delta. Assoc. Am. Geogrs., Annals, 32:149–254.
1954 Alluvial morphology of Anatolian rivers. Assoc. Am. Geogrs., Annals, 44:363–391.
1958 Geological geomorphology. Geol. Soc. Am., Bull. 69:1–22.

Sternberg, H. O.
1956 A contribution to the geomorphology of the False River area, Louisiana. La. State Univ. dissertation (obtainable on microfilm, L. S. U. Library).
1959a Radiocarbon dating as applied to a problem of Amazonian morphology. 17 Internat. Geogr. Congress (Brazil), C. R. 2:399–424.
1959b (with R. J. Russell) Fracture patterns in the Amazon and Mississippi valleys. 17 Internat. Geogr. Congress (Brazil), C. R. 2:380–385.

Sundborg, A.
1956 The river Klarälven: a study of fluvial processes. Univ. Uppsala, Geogr. Inst., Meddell, Ser. A, Nr. 115, and Geogr. Annaler 38:127–316.

Thompson, P. W. (see Vogel)

Vogel, H. D.
1933 (with P. W. Thompson) Flow in river bends. Civ. Engineering, May, 1933: 266–268.

Welder, F. A.
1955 Deltaic processes in Cubits Gap area, Plaquemines Parish, Louisiana. La. State Univ. dissertation, 119 pp. + 9 pl. (Univ. Microfilms, Ann Arbor, diss. abstr. 15:255), and in abbreviated form, Processes of deltaic sedimentation in the Lower Mississippi River, La. State Univ. Coastal Studies Inst. Tech. Rept. 12, 90 pp. (obtainable on microfilm, L. S. U. Library).

3 / COASTAL MORPHOLOGY

A statement made many years ago by a distinguished astronomer left a lasting impression on me. It was to the effect that upon retirement he would never look through another telescope nor be concerned with his specialty. But he realized that he would not be happy unless engaged in some program of scientific research. To prepare himself for retirement he was becoming an expert on a biological problem. The whole idea seemed so sensible that I decided to follow suit, but in a less drastic way. I would discontinue working on rivers, flood plains, and deltas, and concentrate on sea coasts.

In 1956, I judged that time for the change had arrived, so embarked on a completely new project; the investigation of possible relationships between mineral composition and beach morphology. The Lesser Antilles would be the first objective because that island arc exhibits not only volcanic and organic beaches, as do true oceanic islands, but also quartz-sand beaches, a characteristic of continental shores. My record since then has been that of plugging along on the original objective but finding interesting problems that have diverted me into additional investigations. On the island of St. Lucia I was detoured into a study that lasted about five years—inquiry into the characteristics and origin of beach rock (Russell,

1959 and 1962; Russell and McIntire, 1965a). Field work on beach rock took me to various parts of the Mediterranean, to coasts of both northern and southern Africa, to various Pacific and Indian Ocean islands, to New Zealand, and to both the east and west coasts of Australia. One of my most instructive experiences was visiting Cocos-Keeling, the first atoll described by Charles Darwin.

As I gained increasing familiarity with sea coasts, it became more and more apparent that my break with riverine and delta studies was not as drastic as I anticipated. The beach became something closely related to bars along a meandering river. Despite impressive superficial contrasts, the two have in common many similar hydraulic problems (Einstein, 1948). But the change was agreeable. Coastal field work is both interesting and presents new challenges. While one may remain something of a specialist in matters of process, he has to become a generalist on broader questions and he encounters many biological problems.

CLASSIFICATION

Much of the literature on sea coasts is concerned with classification of shoreline types, but to me this is both unfortunate and premature. Taxonomy should follow, rather than precede, the acquisition of more precise and factual information than we now possess. Much of my last nine years has been spent in reconnaissance, in order to acquire background and to identify problems worth investigating. I think that we know altogether too little about coasts to line up examples and shove them into appropriate pigeonholes.

The "classical" classification of shorelines (Johnson, 1919) was quite well discredited by the time I became seriously interested in coastal morphology. It was apparent that the shores of Scandinavia, although displaying all characteristics of classical submergence, flank one of the most rapidly rising landmasses on earth. In 1937, I had found that the delta of the Rhône was not an axis separating areas of submerging from emerging land, although the shorelines to the west display all conventional characteristics of emergence, and those to the east of submergence (Russell, 1942). The whole coast of the Gulf of Lions exhibits Quaternary terraces that have not been tilted longitudinally, as they should be in order to sustain the theory upon which the classification was based. Instead, these depositional surfaces cross the region horizontally.

Glacio-eustatic changes of level between land and sea resulting from the melting of continental ice has raised the level of the oceans by some 450 feet during the Recent rise of sea level (Russell, 1964a). This fact is responsible for drowning practically all sea coasts, so that they are almost universally submergent. That some coasts are smooth in outline, exhibit barrier islands fronting linear lagoons, and display other features considered as proof of emergence according to classical theory is really a demonstration of the efficacy of wave attack and related shore processes to wear away headlands and to fill embayments, provided that the rocks under attack are unconsolidated (Russell, 1957). The classical shorelines of emergence occur only where the sea encounters Quaternary, Tertiary, or other rock that is poorly bound by cement or for other reasons lacks induration. Where resistant, durable rock is exposed to wave impact, the forces of marine attack are almost powerless to change shorelines. The full impact of Atlantic wave and swell beats ineffectively against the high limestone cliff of Cape St. Vincent in southwestern Portugal (Pl. 13) and against crystalline rock in the vicinity of Rio de Janeiro without cutting an appreciable notch. The rugged, rockbound coasts retain practically unaltered evidence of drowning. Their rock is indurated and durable.

PLATE 13. *(Above)* Limestone cliff of Cape St. Vincent, Portugal, is practically unaltered by wave erosion since sea level reached its present stand.

PLATE 14. *(Below)* Peak Head area, near Albany, Western Australia, is typical of crystalline rock coasts.

PLATE 15. Steeply dipping, highly indurated sandstones of late Paleozoic age form the treacherous "needles" of Cape Agulhas, the southern tip of Africa. These highly irregular needles extend far seaward and have wrecked innumerable ships.

PLATE 16. Horizontal Triassic and Cretaceous sandstones, Bluff Point, near the mouth of Murchison River, Western Australia.

PLATE 17. Unconsolidated sand coast, Torreneuvo, Spain.

Were I to forecast the basis upon which a sound classification of shorelines might be based, I would first think
in terms of lithology. Crystalline-rock coasts, for example, exhibit striking similarities, regardless of climatic,
vegetational, or other environmental contrasts. Many
parts of the coast of Scandinavia, southwestern Australia (Pl. 14), South Africa, and other crystalline-rock
areas that I have visited exhibit similar domed surfaces,
effects of large-scale rock spalling, and conspicuous joint
control. These coasts, including shorelines near Rio de
Janeiro, display forms that are closely akin to those that
would be developed in the Sierra Nevada were sea level
to rise high enough to submerge the floor of Yosemite
Valley and waves were to beat against the face of Half
Dome.

Horizontally bedded limestone, massive limestone,
moderately or steeply dipping indurated sedimentary or
metamorphic rocks, (Pls. 15 and 16) and, of course,
poorly consolidated sediments (Pl. 17) offer possibilities
as major divisions in a shoreline classification. Lesser
categories might include factors such as the presence or
absence of pronounced longshore drift, exposure to persistent swell or high-energy waves, widths of continental
shelves, organisms present, and a host of other controls
that it seems premature to enumerate.

CHANGES OF LEVEL

Were most continental ice to melt, complicated effects
would be experienced by the earth's crust. Relief from
load would cause some land areas to rise, as is now the
case in much of eastern Canada and adjacent parts of
the United States, Scandinavia, and elsewhere. Increased
water load would depress the floors of ocean basins. But,
the net rise of sea level along continental and island
coasts should be approximately 200 feet. (Ahlmann
[1953] calculates 200 feet but does not evaluate isostatic

effects. These may be counterbalanced by greater volume of ice on Antarctica, as suggested by observations
during and following the International Geophysical
year.) Were this to happen, Postglacial time would have
arrived. It is inappropriate to say that it is here now because the area of continental ice and its volume are about
one-third that during any glacial maximum. By the same
token, I feel that the only reason for recognizing the
Quaternary as a subdivision of geological time is because
it differs from the Tertiary in being characterized by the
presence of large continental ice masses (Russell, 1950).
Prior to the initiation of the Quaternary I question
whether there were conspicuous continental shelves and
believe ocean level stood something like 200 feet higher
than it does today.

Eustatic changes of level, for many years, were regarded in terms of a progressive though intermittent
lowering sea level, and commonly were explained as resulting from subsidence of ocean floors, mainly of the
Pacific (Russell, 1964a). This thesis is accepted by some
people today, but has been discarded by most students
in favor of glacio-eustatic theory for changes occurring
during the Quaternary, the last chapter in the record of
earth history.

The gradual acceptance of the Ice Age has been out-
lined very well by Flint (1947 and 1957). Although Hut-
ton (Playfair, 1802) was one of the first, toward the end
of the eighteenth century, to recognize that erratic
boulders removed far from their source bedrock had been
transported by glaciers, and Bernhardi (1832),Charpen-
tier (1841), and others anticipated him, it remained for
Agassiz to present a glacial theory in terms that resulted
in widespread interest and somewhat general acceptance. His paper was read in 1837 and published in full in
1840. What I regard as an example of a great display of
scientific acumen was the publication in 1842 of Charles
Maclaren's statement concerning the effects of continen-

tal glaciation on stands of sea level (1842). Under assumptions that he regarded as reasonable, Maclaren suggested that the depression of sea level must have been about 800 feet during the maximum of ice cover and that returning meltwater had resulted in recovery to a level about 100 feet lower than the pre-glacial stand.

Iu 1872, Tylor reduced the estimate of lowering to 600 feet. Penck (1894) calculated lowerings amounting to a range between almost nothing and 650 feet, depending on varying assumptions as to the thickness of ice cover, but thought that the evidence of Pacific atolls demanded a drop of 300 feet. This value was adopted by Daly (1910) and most of his successors. However, Nansen in 1922, and Ramsay in 1930 estimated the drop as about 485 feet. Our own studies suggest that it was 450 feet, prior to the initiation of the Recent, a time we regard as coincident with the last major rise of sea level, together with a stillstand of about 3,000 years at close to present-day stage. I have suggested that the first evidence of lowering sea level, or initiation of the Quaternary, dates from at least 1.8 million years, and that five major fluctuations have occurred since then (Russell, 1964b). Our latest evidence suggests that the estimate is too conservative. The time intervals between fluctuations have decreased progressively. Our field work during the last four years indicates that at least three of the four higher stands of Pleistocene seas roughly approximated today's sea level. The last high stand was about 20 feet higher, the next older about 30 feet, the oldest we have determined at this time approximates today's level. The stand following the first main glacial stage presumably was somewhat lower. At least we have been unable to find evidence of it on any stable coast we have examined and we believe that our sampling has been sufficiently intense that if this oldest Quaternary stand was higher than today's level we would have discovered it. We certainly are not satisfied with negative evidence, however, so will continue our investigation.

The rate at which sea level rose during the Recent was so rapid that coastal landforms in consolidated rock have not changed appreciably. As a general principle all "hard-rock" topography near coasts must be regarded in terms of a geomorphology developed during low stands of Quaternary seas. For something on the order of two million years the sculpturing of ice-free surfaces ordinarily proceeded toward base levels well below those today. Coastal valleys cut to these low levels accumulated alluvial fill each time sea level rose to a position approximating that of today, but the hills flanking them were relatively unchanged.

In unconsolidated rock or in the case of depositional coastal landforms, such as marshes and tidal flats, we must think primarily in terms of events of the last eight thousand years, during the stillstand and a few thousand years preceding it. Eight thousand years ago sea level stood about twenty-nine feet lower than it does today (Coleman and Smith, 1964). It is probably coincidental that this happens to approximate the maximum depth where waves are effective in entraining loose sediments, except under extraordinary storm conditions.

While my main interests in coastal morphology, like those in geomorphology in general, have been concerned with depositional forms and processes, eustasy studies required that I pay some attention to erosional forms (Russell, 1963). The literature covering changes of level is crammed with misinterpretations of evidence for identifying sea stands. The usual criterion is that of measuring the elevation of some bench and this results in publishing the value as a stand of sea level. It is astonishing to examine the evidence in the field. Most benches occur in horizontally bedded rock, commonly in limestone. Some, as near Santa Cruz, California, may depend on the level of the water table. If coastal erosion has been rapid a bench should form close to sea level because rocks in the zone of aeration, above the water table, are more readily attacked and removed than those below, in

PLATE 18. The planed bedrock below the water table is the same as that of the high sea cliff, Praiha Post de Mois, Portugal.

the zone of cementation (Pl. 18). Although one may witness bench formation at differing levels as being in progress today, the enthusiastic searcher for higher sea stands is likely to disregard that fact. Whether the benches occur at elevations higher than the level to which oceans would rise were all continental ice to melt ordinarily is deemed immaterial.

Few people who stand on the rim of the Grand Canyon in Arizona, would postulate halts in the downcutting of the Colorado River as a means of explaining the Tonto or other benches within the canyon. But when the equivalent problem faces coastal morphologists, they commonly have come up with essentially that explanation; each bench supposedly represents a stand of sea level.

Our own determinations of high stands of Quaternary seas have been based almost exclusively on elevations of reef-flat deposits, or other organic accumulations. On the

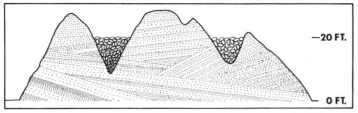

Fig. 26. Sketch showing relationships between oyster-shell deposits and complexly eroded eolianite, Umhloti, Natal.

coast of Natal, at Umhloti, not far north of Durban, for example, in a place where the coastal rock is a complexly dissected eolianite, we found many ravines filled with *in situ* deposits of shells of a species of oyster that is said to be extinct (Fig. 26). All of these deposits rise to a common elevation. None was higher. This evidence we regard as a valid indication of a sea stand. As we had found reef flats at the same elevation on the stable granitic islands of Seychelles, and for long distances on the coast of Western Australia, we felt confident in our belief that we were dealing with a significant stand of Quaternary sea level. On evidence of this substantial nature we identified levels at approximately twenty and thirty feet. In 1964 we found that they occur not only around the shores of the Indian Ocean but also on a number of Antillean islands: Jamaica, Puerto Rico, Antigua, Barbuda, Guadeloupe, Dominica, and Grenada. While we have uranium-series dates and other reasons to believe that the twenty-foot level dates from a sea stand of at least 80,000 or even 130,000 years ago, and the thirty-foot, at least 227,000 years ago, we hopefully await some means of isotope dating that will fix their antiquities more precisely (Russell, 1964b).

BEACH TYPES

Beaches do not provide useful criteria for determining Quaternary sea levels, nor do scattered shells of mollusks even though they may be restricted to a narrow vertical zone when alive. Several miles east of Port Hedland,

Western Australia, I have observed shells that have been washed back among sand dunes at times of storm to settle as high as twenty-five feet above sea level. And along the coast north of Cape Cuvier, north of Carnarvon, Western Australia, Pleistocene beaches exhibit altitudinal variation of a similar amount behind reef flats that occur consistently at an elevation of about twenty feet (Fig. 27).

Beaches, however, are natural objects of study to one who is interested in the morphology of sea coasts. Beach investigations rank foremost among the current research projects of the Coastal Studies Institute of Louisiana State University. We are interested in their origins and processes involved in their morphology, rather than attempts to categorize them by types. Taxonomic considerations are tempting because there is such a wide spectrum of appearances between the coarse shingle beaches of England and the silt beaches of Louisiana.

Although Chesil Bank (Fig. 28) has been one of the most investigated beaches on earth, it remains much of an enigma (Steers, 1942). Reduction in shingle size from that of cobbles up to about five inches in longest diameter near Portland (Pl. 19), to that of marbles at Bridport (Pl. 20), eighteen miles to the west, indicates a source to the east, but rocks that outcrop on Portland

Fig. 27. Relationship between low-tide level, reef flats, and beaches typical of the coast north of Cape Cuvier, Western Australia, during both the Recent and latest Pleistocene high stands of sea level.

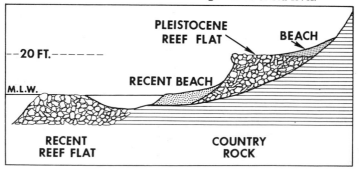

Bill or its vicinity do not suggest where such a tremendous volume of flint shingle came from and the longshore drift today is not in the appropriate direction. At its Portland end the accumulation rises forty-three feet above high water level and Professor Clarence Kidson, who was with me in the field, said that by diving he found that the deposit continues to a depth of fifty feet or more with unbroken slope seaward and without any sign of change from shingle sizes displayed above. One may speculate as to whether this is an extremely old accumulation, derived from some concentration of flint shingle during the Tertiary, or at least prior to the origin of the Strait of Dover, that has remained little altered during the fluctuations of Quaternary sea level. There is every reason to believe that Chesil Bank long has served as an effective barrier protecting a lagoon called The Fleet, and low, flat land to its rear.

Louisiana beaches, although consisting of little material larger than coarse silt, are also protective. As in the case of Chesil Bank, or beaches generally, they are accumulations of the coarsest material locally available to wave-current transport. Shells, solid pieces of flotsam,

Fig. 28. Chesil Bank, The Fleet, low flat areas, and hills in the vicinity of Portland, Dorset, England.

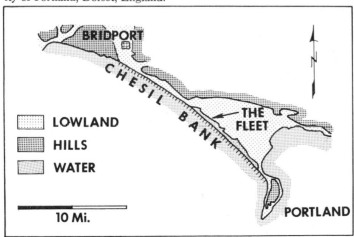

PLATE 19. Shingle near the Portland end of Chesil Bank, Dorset, England.

PLATE 20. Shingle near the Bridport end of Chesil Bank, Dorset England.

some fine sand, and much silt provide an armor that holds in place under- or back-lying fine silt, clay, and organic marsh deposits.

When a hurricane strikes the Louisiana coast directly, it crosses such a wide, shallow continental shelf that an accompanying wave builds to heights commonly of six to eight feet, and in the case of Hurricane Audrey, in 1957, to thirteen feet. The Audrey wave not only flooded marshes and cheniers for up to thirty miles inland but also removed most of the beach (Morgan, Nichols and Wright, 1958; Chamberlain, 1959). Lacking their protective armor the underlying deposits were eroded rapidly and the shoreline retreated at an accelerated rate for about four years, after which a new beach accumulated and rates of erosion and accretion along the coast returned to those of pre-Audrey time.

A curious incident of coastal modification that accompanied the arrival of the Audrey wave was the formation of a mud arc over two miles long, and at a maximum about 2,000 feet wide (Fig. 29). The mass was crescentic, convex gulfward. Its horns were shifted inland, as

Fig. 29. Eastern of two mud arcs, Vermilion Parish, Louisiana, formed by Hurricane Audrey, June 27, 1957. Parts of a new mudflat were lifted and drifted landward to be deposited on top of beach and marsh sediments (after Morgan, Nichols, and Wright).

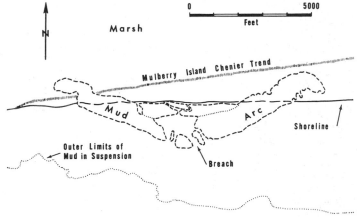

much as 1,200 feet over the marsh surface. Outflowing water associated with subsiding flood level breached the central part of the arc, but its ends remain today as deposits of dense clay up to 2 feet thick that blanket underlying marsh deposits. The mud-arc clay was lifted bodily out of the post-1947 mudflat described in the first chapter. Although the new clay layer is as permanent as the deposits it covers, the effect of clay removal from the coastal mudflat was trivial. Within a year the mudflat regained its pre-storm dimensions. A similar, but unstudied, mud arc was created a dozen miles to the west. Others have been found in fossil condition.

Between the extreme examples of Chesil Bank and the beaches of Louisiana we find that most beaches are composed of mineral or rock particles in which sand or gravel predominate, or that they consist of organic debris. So many of them display quartz sand that dwellers along medium or high latitude shores of continents are likely to believe that all sand is composed of quartz. Tropical ocean island inhabitants, on the other hand, recognize that black or greenish beaches are derived from rock, whereas white or pale reddish beaches are accumulations of shell or coral debris. There is, of course, a tremendous variety in beach materials, some black-sand continental beaches are worth mining for their titanium or other metal content, some are composed almost entirely of glass shards, derived from explosive volcanoes, but in most cases the material present in a beach is either hard and abrasion resistant or else is locally available in considerable quantity, as for example, the tests of foraminifera, the spicules of echinoids, the plates of brittle stars, or the fragments of the calcareous green alga, *Halimeda*, on tropical beaches we have studied.

In form, beaches vary from deposits in small pockets or coves, commonly concave seaward in pattern, to linear strips over a hundred miles in length, as along the coast of Morocco between Agadir and the Dra (Pl. 21), or

PLATE 21. Plage Blanche, 16 miles long and about 2,000 feet wide, near Foum el Oued, the southern point of the coast of Morocco, is one of many long, straight beaches along the Atlantic coast of Africa.

along the coast of southern Texas. Many long, straight beaches are anchored at either end by some rocky headland or even a submerged deposit of clay that has resisted erosional removal by waves (Russell, 1958). Some beaches form spits or have shapes determined by current directions and velocity changes.

Beach profiles also vary considerably and one may well take them into account in estimating how exhausted he may become after walking along the shore for several miles. In most cases he will find that flat beaches are far easier to walk upon than steeper ones and if interested may observe the reasons why. Steep-fronted beaches typically are composed of coarser particles, more loosely arranged. Finer sand is commonly firm and better packed. Beaches composed of fine sand are ordinarily flatter and if platy or tabular particles predominate, the sand in all probability will be much firmer than if composed of rounded grains. These characteristics are associated with mineral composition to a considerable degree, but although I have been measuring beach slopes, collecting, and analyzing samples for several years, my original coastal project is far from solved. It is complicated and too many interesting diversions along the way have attracted me by the lure of presenting problems offering a possibility of new and apparently significant conclusions.

BEACH PROCESSES

There is incomplete agreement about the definition of beach, or the terminology for describing its parts. To the populace, and editors of Webster's dictionary, a beach is an area, while to a scientist it is a deposit. Popularly, it is the area exposed during lowest tide, but I prefer to think of it as consisting of two main parts, as suggested by Bagnold (1940), an upper beach which is exposed most of the time, and a· lower beach that extends outward as a submarine feature as far as its sedimentary particles are being moved about by wave currents (Fig. 30). Each of the parts is ordinarily concave upward and between them there is likely to be a linear upward convexity, near the *step*. This is located approximately at the outermost limit of wave backwash during low tide. A person wading toward the surf commonly finds that the step is somewhat steeper than the beach above or below and that it is characterized by the presence of coarser material. The upward concavity of both the upper and lower beach is commonly interrupted by minor irregularities. There may be distinct *berms*, or ephemeral terraces, that mark times of higher wave energy and limits of swash cover, beach cusps (Russell and McIntire, 1965*b*), and other topographic forms on the upper beach. The lower beach commonly exhibits a wavy profile seaward, resulting from the presence of migrating submerged bars with troughs between them. When exposed at low tide these are called ridges and runnels.

When swimming at Daytona, or many other Atlantic

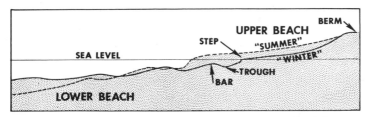

Fig. 30. Beach terminology. Changes in profile occur both because sand is shifted landward and seaward with variations in wave energy and because in many places sand moves as bars that migrate parallel to the shoreline.

beaches, one may encounter a vigorous and unpleasant longshore drift of sand that peppers the skin. But on crossing the first main line of breakers, one ordinarily finds pleasant, clear water. This common experience points up the fact that the key to beach morphology lies within the surf zone. It is there that turbulence reaches greatest intensity, that bottom sediment is entrained most rapidly, and load is provided for forward transport by wave uprush toward the inner limit of the swash zone or carried seaward by wave or tidal currents.

When wave energy is high the zone of sediment entrainment widens across the upper beach, to erode sand or shingle and transport it seaward in backwash current. With loss of volume the upper beach is lowered, flattened, and in some cases may become covered by a residual pavement of coarse material (Russell and McIntire, 1965*b*). In this way *winter beach* conditions are established. Although lesser volumes and more flatness characterize upper beaches during winters, especially if that season is stormy and brings high-energy waves, the tendency toward establishing a winter beach arises any time when heavy swell appears or wave steepness increases. In contrast is the more voluminous, wider, more steeply fronted *summer beach* that tends to become established when waves lower and flatten. Sediment is then entrained in the surf zone, transported forward in the swash and much of it is deposited. Deposition occurs because

turbulence decreases as velocity lowers and finally
reaches a dead period at the height of maximum uprush.
During backwash milder turbulence is incapable of entraining much sediment and seaward flow is comparatively gentle under low-energy conditions. If the beach
consists of shingle much uprush water disappears by
percolation.

In order to investigate the reasons for changes in beach
morphology in a thorough way, under natural conditions,
the Coastal Studies Institute has engaged in an experi-
mental program on the Outer Banks of North Carolina,
not far north of Cape Hatteras. Our experience on that
beach spans more than ten years. We chose a site where
there is minimum complication related to the presence
of inlets, where beach stratification is clearly evident,
and the range in size of sediment particles is large. In
our first attempt the pier we used was washed away after
twenty-six days of observation, by the storm of March,
1962 (Dolan, 1965). We returned to another pier in Sep-
tember, 1964, and recorded observations until the following June. This phase of the investigation was concerned primarily with beach geometry and measuring
values of factors which we presume are associated with
observed changes.

We photographed on color film, each hour around the
clock, the changes taking place on a monumented beach
about 200 feet square, from October, 1964, to June, 1965
(Pl. 22). We also obtained 2,000 feet of 16 mm film by
means of time-lapse photography at times of highly vari-
able beach conditions. We profiled sand levels at the
ends of 341 tidal cycles and hourly during 145 cycles.
Using plugs of colored sand near thin scaled rods of
known elevation, we determined to the nearest 0.01 foot
the amount of sand removed during each rising tide and
conducted an intensive sampling program within the
monumented area of the sediment deposited during each
falling tide for 145 tides. Wind speed and direction were

PLATE 22. Monumented study beach, Outer Banks, North Carolina, at a time when cusps were forming after a period of high wave energy. As energy levels drop the waves will transport sand shoreward and deposit some of it above the winter-beach gravel that covers most of the foreground.

recorded continuously between November and June. Air temperature 20 feet above sea level and water temperature at an average depth of 12 feet were recorded continuously between October and December, and between March and June. Tidal range was recorded continuously between October and June. During each of 145 tides from four to twelve records were kept of still-water level. Wave direction was recorded four times during each of these tides, and the speed of uprush across the swash zone was recorded from four to six times per tide. With the cooperation of the United States Army, Coastal Engineering Research Center, we recorded on magnetic tape the arrival time and height of every wave that passed between November and June. Four minutes of the record were printed on paper tape every four hours.

This enumeration has been tedious, but it suggests the complexity of the problem we face in our basic research on beach morphology. We estimate that it will require at least three years for analysis of the observations of this phase of the study with benefit of a competent staff of analysts and excellent computer facilities.

While our analyses are proceeding in Baton Rouge, we are carrying out cooperative projects with the hydraulics and electronics laboratories of the University of Uppsala, Sweden, to develop theory and instrumentation needed before we return to field observations that will take us beyond matters such as beach geometry and parameter recording, into a far more critical examination of turbulence processes within the surf zone, as well as recording bar migrations, both transverse and parallel to the strandline.

This and most of our other programs have been supported financially by the Geography Branch of the Office of Naval Research. The Coast and Geodetic Survey helped finance work on the Outer Banks. We hope that this study will yield basic data needed by engineers who are charged with designing defenses against the sea and provide morphologists with a much better understanding of beach processes.

In the second century, B.C., Attalus Philadelphus was convinced by engineers that the construction of a mole would end an annoying silting problem in the harbor of Ephesus. But after its construction the harbor was promptly ruined by accelerated deposition (Strabo, circa 7 B.C.). Similar mistakes have been common in southern California, Japan, and elsewhere in recent years. It is high time that scientists supply engineers with more adequate basic information on shore processes.

SAND SUPPLY

My reconnaissance investigations on many of the world's coasts lead to the conclusion that the majority of beaches are diminishing in volume. This unfortunate circumstance is coupled with a rising demand for beach sand caused by rapidly increasing populations and a revolution in building practices. Wood, earth, brick, stone, and other traditional building materials are being replaced by concrete. Sand loss was first noticed and regarded as an acute problem on recreation beaches close to large

centers of population, where expensive nourishment programs have been in effect for some decades. But now it
is recognized that the effects are more widespread. Practically all seaboard countries have prohibited or strictly
regulated the mining of beach sand during the last fif-
teen years or so. Beach sand is ordinarily clean, hard, and
relatively free from organic impurities, and thus is an
excellent aggregate for concrete. River sand is less valu-
able as a rule and what is most unfortunate is the fact
that desert sand is ordinarily so well rounded and polished that it will not adhere firmly to cement.

The examination of sand dunes along sea coasts points
up one morphological effect of sand loss from beaches.
Higher, older dunes ordinarily contain much larger sand
volumes than dunes now accumulating. The older dunes
are likely to be fixed by well-established growths of vegetation. Their sand is more oxidized and leached, and
hence they appear gray or yellowish in comparison to
the fresh, white sand of present-day emplacement. This
reduction in surplus beach sand for dune nourishment is
a consequence of the diminishing volume of beaches.

The reduction in sand volume probably originated as
a result of the Recent stillstand in sea level. As long as
seas were rising rapidly from their pre-Recent low level
or at a rate of about eight to twelve inches per century
as stillstand was approached, they encroached on old
coastal plains and new surfaces were being flooded.
These provided sources of sand, which, together with
other relatively coarse material, was transported shoreward by wave action. Beaches increased in volume as
they were pushed inland and gently upward across old
and invaded coastal plains. Some surplus sand was blown
off to accumulate as dunes. But when stillstand was attained new sand supplies were no longer encountered.
Beaches and the older dunes had attained maximum volume. With continuation of the stillstand, beaches lost
volume and much less sand was available to nourish

dunes. The older dunes became stabilized, but the abundance and volumes of mobile new dunes dropped appreciably.

If we consider the whole beach-dune system, we see the reason for sand loss. During most of the time little volumetric change occurs. Sand is transported seaward during ordinary storms when winter-beach conditions are being established, only to return to the beach after wave energy drops and a trend is established toward summer-beach development. But during intense storms, when extreme beach erosion occurs, some sand is carried seaward to depths of more than five or six fathoms, from which it is not likely to be returned to the system. In areas where the tidal range is extreme another significant factor is introduced; the currents generated during the ebb of spring tides constitute a far more effective agency of seaward sand transport than occurs during the landward movement associated with flow tides.

TIDAL FLATS

Although I had witnessed tidal bores in the Bay of Fundy and on the lower Amazon, and in 1948 became interested in the effects of extreme tidal range on the North Sea coasts of France and Belgium, I did not consider undertaking a detailed study of tidal flats until 1961, when McIntire and I witnessed beautiful examples on Australian coasts.

Many Australians hold strong convictions. They become belligerent if one denies that their beer is the world's best or their sharks the most voracious. Some will argue heatedly that the Ord is the fourth largest river on earth, and many will tell you that tidal range is a function of latitude; the lower the latitude the higher the range. For their own continent this is very much the case. Ranges of spring tides are low along the southern coast, amount to about four or five feet near Sydney or Fre-

mantle, attain up to twenty-five feet in parts of Queensland or on the northwest coast east of Onslow, and reach
a maximum range of fifty-two feet at Wyndham on the
northern coast, about 300 miles southwest of Darwin.
That the range is inconsequential along the north coast
of Java, in still lower latitude, is either unknown or dis-
regarded by most Australians.

In 1961, McIntire and I saw much of the east coast of
Australia and visited practically every point accessible
to automobile travel between Cape Leeuwin, the southwest tip of the continent, and Darwin (Russell and Mc-
Intire, 1966). In Queensland we found an interesting
delta which we would have investigated with enthusiasm
but our schedule did not permit the delay. In 1965, however, the Coastal Studies Institute sent a party of three,
each with several years of experience in delta research,
to spend six months studying the Burdekin Delta.

On the west coast the distance by road from Perth to
Darwin is about 2,800 miles, but we actually traveled
over 4,100 because we took so many side trips between
the highway and the coast. Again, time did not permit
long stops for studies of interesting problems, particularly as we were being advised, time and again, that extremely poor and possibly impassable roads lay ahead.
In 1963, McIntire and I returned with Henry V. Howe
and Jonathan Sauer to examine tidal flats at places selected eighteen months previously. As we had less than
three months for Australian field work that year, our investigations were concentrated in two localities; one, the
vicinity of Darwin, where the spring tidal range is about
thirty feet, and the other near Port Hedland, where we
found it to be about ten feet higher.

Studying tidal flats is both interesting and exacting. It
is necessary to arrive at a site a few days before a spring
tide, to make detailed plans. When the day of maximum
range comes, you arrive at a selected locality in the dark
of the morning. As soon as dawn breaks and there is suffi-

cient light, you walk as rapidly as possible across the flat in order to reach its outer edge before the tide turns. When it does, you begin surveying a section shoreward, ahead of the rising water. Then, rather late in the afternoon, at a time depending on the slope and width of the flat, you survey a section from the beach, seaward in the wake of ebbing water, until you judge that declining daylight will last just long enough to permit return to the beach. You really have one critical day for observing the outer part of the flat, ordinarily a day or so after new or full moon. The day preceding and that following are fairly instructive, but the remaining days of the month had better be used for other purposes.

In Australia we found that the most interesting contrast between tidal flats is related to the sand volume present on adjacent beaches. Where there is a deficiency the flats are extremely interesting biologically. Sponges, corals, coralline algae, tube-building worms, sea anemonies, and a host of other organisms thrive near the edge of the flat (Pl. 23). In a short distance inland there is a

PLATE 23. Corals, sponges, and other organisms living at the seaward edge of a tidal flat, Port Hedland, Western Australia.

belt where large tridactnas and other mollusks predominate, with many pools where eels, squid, octopuses, and
occasional stone fish and other animals are concentrated.
Toward the shore are belts characterized by contrasting
colonies of algae, and distinct zones in which gooseneck
barnacles, mussels, and other mollusca live in well-
defined ecological associations. If some sand is present,
molluscan populations increase in the outer part of the
lower beach and shoreward. On bedrock above the
beach, but below the limit of extreme high tide, green
algae, rock oysters, chitons, balanus-type barnacles and
small gastropods prevail. On the tidal flats of Cocos-
Keeling and Viti Levu, Fiji, we have encountered areas
where the most consipicuous animals are sea cucumbers
and jellyfish. We are anxious to return to sand-deficient
tidal flats with a party including a taxonomic algologist
and a zoologist sufficiently acquainted with the taxonomy of corals, worms, and other tidal-flat animals to supplement our studies.

Where surplus sand exists the biology is less interesting but we found morphological changes occurring at
impressive rates. The flats off Casuarina Beach, near Darwin, or off Beautiful Pool, about five miles east of Port
Hedland, appear monotonous and, on first blush, unex-
citing. Gradients are gentle, low ridge and runnel topography exists on a broad scale. The entire flat is part of
the lower beach. Clams, crabs, and flat echinoids are
abundant and practically all pools contain octpods and
sea anemonies, but our focus was on physical change,
rather than biological associations.

On two occasions, I have observed the turn of the tide
when almost absolute calm existed both in air and sea.
This happened once near Darwin; later I was to see it
at Keimouth, on the boundary between Cape of Good
Hope Colony and Transkei, South Africa. The start of
rising tide is marked by the arrival of distinct bores, of
small height, possibly only an inch or less, but as the

front of each little wave of translation passed, the water became higher by a distinct increment; the height of the bore. This fact eludes an observer if waves even a few inches high are present.

We devoted as much time as possible to observing the creation of new ripple marks both when we saw the bores and at times when low waves obscured them. The ripple marks appear almost immediately after the sand is covered by landward flowing currents of water. They are sharp-crested, straight, parallel the front of the rising tide, and are spaced as closely as six inches and as widely as ten inches apart on flats where we saw them forming. Seaward ripple-mark slopes were packed somewhat more firmly than slopes facing landward. The troughs between them accumulate very fine debris, mainly of algal origin. This fine, light debris is readily entrained and whisked up in turbulent plumes with each passing wave to be carried landward and deposited in new troughs. We gained the impression that most of the regular ripple marks we observed on tidal flats are formed and grow in height, up to from one to three inches as a rule, when the tide is rising. The zone where a new set of ripple marks originates thus gradually widens toward the shore during flood tide. Unrelated to this orderly process are megaripples that form during falling tide, particularly where strong currents exist, as out from estuarine embayments and river mouths.

The effects of currents generated during extreme tidal ebbing were particularly interesting on Casuarina Beach, a short distance south of Lee Point, near Darwin. As ripple marks ordinarily parallel the strandline, they tend to become active channels for flow of water in that direction as the tide falls. But this direction doesn't satisfy the demands of gravity, so ripples are breached at some places and flow is established seaward at gaps eroded across their crests (Fig. 31). Toward the upper beach this effect may not result in any very significant modification,

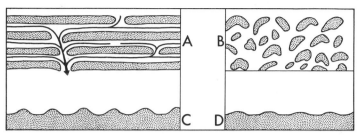

Fig. 31. (A) directions of flow along and across ripple marks during falling tide; (B) appearance of ripple marks after they have undergone considerable erosional modification; (C and D) vertical cross-sections of ripple marks such as are shown in plan sketches above each.

but below the springline, about at the level of high neap tide, where flow of groundwater reinforces tidal water volumes (Pl. 24), the erosion is more pronounced and ripples may be chopped into segments as small as a foot or so in length and exhibit seaward bowing of their crests on sides of all breaching channels, so that the shape of each segment becomes somewhat crescentic, with horns pointing seaward. For an hour or two after the turn toward ebb tide the rate of fall is comparatively slow but later on accelerates. For that reason the volume of water flowing seaward increases and its velocity becomes much higher about two hours after the inner part of the tidal flat is uncovered. Ripple marks farther out, say about half way across the flat, become highly distorted or even eroded to a degree where their previous locations are evident only in patterns of grain-size distribution (Pl. 25).

Characteristics of ripple mark modification are duplicated on a much grander scale in ridge and runnel topography. The runnels become wide pools between dry ridge crests, but as long as the flow of water in the pools tends to parallel the strandline a condition of instability is being created. Pools fill to the level of low points along ridges, breach them, and empty their waters into seaward pools at a somewhat lower level. Where pool width may reach several hundred feet and water filling occurs to depths such as three feet, the short-lived channels

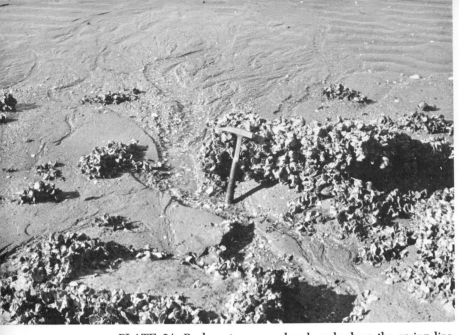

PLATE 24. Rock oysters cover .beach rock along the spring line, where groundwater flows out to cross ripple marks, Beautiful Pool, near Port Hedland, Western Australia.

PLATE 25. Severely deformed and eroded ripple marks, Lee Point, Australia.

across ridges become ,vigorous channels in which flow may be torrential.

Of common occurrence is the appearance of antidunes along these streams. Starting at a time when the water surface is relatively smooth, one observes that within a minute or so the surface suddenly becomes riffled, then the riffle heights increase. Rapidly developing bed roughness increases turbulence tremendously. At the peak of the process, antidunes (Pl. 26) form because entrainment of sand is extremely rapid on downcurrent dune faces below ripples and deposition is correspondingly rapid on stoss faces, so that while dune crests migrate upcurrent, the transport of sand downcurrent is torrentially rapid. At length the turbulence reaches sufficient intensity to erode and erase a whole series of antidunes almost instantaneously and their sand content is swept seaward, after which the channel bed may be quite flat for a minute or so. Then the process of development and erasure of antidunes is repeated at two or three minute intervals as long as flow remains torrential.

Other evidences of seaward sand transport on tidal flats include kidney-shaped scour pools with concave boundaries toward the shore (Pl. 27). These may have lengths up to three feet and depths of up to nearly a foot. Nothing less than torrential flow could scour them.

Large volumes of sand are lost from ripple marks as shown by their eroded flat crests, deformed shapes, or removal across the zone of maximum velocity of water outflow. Flattening of crests was also observed on some large ridges between runnels that had become completely flooded.

On most tidal flats that we have studied there is a distinct dropoff at the outer edge beyond which wave shapes suggest that depths of several fathoms occur. In no case have we observed indications that sand is being transferred from areas beyond the dropoffs to the flats. On the other hand, we have witnessed the rapidity with

PLATE 26. Antidunes in a narrow channel with torrential flow, Lee Point, Australia. The water flows toward the left, across a ridge. The pick was placed close to the edge of the channel. Crests of waves above antidunes move toward the right.

PLATE 27. Kidney-shaped scour pools eroded by the torrential flow of ebb tide about halfway across the tidal flat, Lee Point, Australia.

which sand moves seaward and is being lost from beach systems.

In retrospect, my experiences in coástal morphology closely parallel those in alluvial morphology. I have concentrated on depositional features because they have not been studied adequately and because they offer such exciting challenges. And my research in both cases turned to the study of processes, and to some extent involved forms relating to Quaternary changes of level between land and sea.

REFERENCES

Agassiz, L.
    1840 Etudes sur les glaciers. Neuchatel (privately printed), 2 vols, 364 pp.
Ahlmann, H. W:son
    1953 Glacier variations and climatic fluctuations. New York (Am. Geogr. Soc.), 51 pp.
Bagnold, R. A.
    1940 Beach formation by waves: some model experiments in a wave tank. Inst. Civ. Engrs., Jour., 15:27–52.
Bernhardi, A.
    1832 Wie kawen die aus dem norden stammenden felsbruchstücke und geschiebe, welche man in Norddeutschland und den benachbarten länder findet, an ihre gegenwärtigen fundort? Jahrb. f. Mineralog., Geognos., und Petrefaktenk. (Heidelberg), 3:257–267.
Chamberlain, J. L.
    1959 Influence of hurricane Audrey on the coastal marsh of southwestern Louisiana. La. State Univ., Coastal Studies Institute, Tech. Rept. 10B, 38 pp. (available on microfilm, L. S. U. Library).
Charpentier, J. de
    1841 Essai sur les glaciers et sur terrain erratique du bassin du Rhône. Lausanne (Marc Ducloux), 363 pp.
Coleman, J. M.
    1964 (with W. G. Smith) Late Recent rise of sea level, Geol. Soc. Am., Bull. 75:833–840.

Daly, R. A.
    1910 Pleistocene glaciation and the coral reef problem.
         Am. Jour. Sci., 4 ser., 30:297–308.
Dolan, R.
    1965 Relationships between nearshore processes and
         beach changes along the Outer Banks of North Caro-
         lina. La. State Univ. dissertation, viii + 51 pp. (avail-
         able on microfilm, Ann Arbor, diss. abstracts).
Einstein, H. A.
    1948 Movement of beach sands by water waves. Am.
         Geophys. Un., Trans. 29:653–655.
Flint, R. F.
    1947 Glacial geology of the Pleistocene epoch. New York
         (John Wiley and Sons), 589 pp.
    1957 Glacial and Pleistocene geology. New York (John
         Wiley and Sons), 533 pp.
D. W. Johnson
    1919 Shore processes and shoreline development. New
         York (John Wiley and Sons), 584 pp.
McIntire, W. G. (see R. J. Russell, 1965a, 1965b, 1966)
Maclaren C.
    1842 The glacial theory of Prof. Agassiz. Am. Jour. Sci.,
         42:346–365.
Morgan, J. P.
    1958 (with L. G. Nichols and M. Wright) Morphological
         effects of hurricane Audrey on the Louisiana Coast,
         La. State Univ. Coastal Studies Inst., Tech. Rept.
         10, 53 p.
Nansen, F.
    1922 The strandflat and isostasy. Videnskp. Skrift., I Mat-
         Naturv. Kl., 11, Kristiania (Hos Jacob Dybwad),
         313 pp.
Nichols, L. G. (see Morgan)
Penck, A.
    1894 Morphologie der erdoberfläche. Stuttgart (J. Engel-
         horn) 2 vols., reference on 2:581, 658–660.
Playfair, J.
    1802 Illustrations of the Huttonian theory of the earth.
         Edinburgh (W. Creech), 528 pp.; reprinted 1956,
         New York (Dover Publs).
Ramsay, W.
    1930 Changes in sea-level resulting from the increase and
         decrease of glaciations. Fennia, 55 No. 5:62.

Russell, R. J.
1942 Geomorphology of the Rhône Delta. Assoc. Am. Geogrs., Annals, 32:149–254.
1950 The Pliocene-Pleistocene boundary in Louisiana. 18 Internat. Geol. Cong. (London), Rept. X:94–96.
1957 Aspects of alluvial morphology. Kon. Ned. Aardrijkskd. Genootsch., 74:377–388.
1958 Long, straight beaches. Eclog. Geol. Helvetiae, 51: 591–598.
1959 Caribbean beach rock observations. Zeitsch. f. Geomorphol., 2:227–236.
1962 Origin of beach rock. Zeitsch. f. Geomorphol., 6:1–6.
1963 Recent recession of tropical cliffy coasts. Science, 139:9–15.
1964a Techniques of eustasy studies. Zeitsch f. Geomorphol, vol. 8, Sonderhft., 8:25–42.
1964b Duration of the Quaternary and its subdivisions. Nat. Acad. Sci., Proc., 52:790–796.
1965a (with W. G. McIntire) Southern hemisphere beach rock. Geogr. Review, 55:17–45.
1965b (with W. G. McIntire) Beach cusps. Geol. Soc. Am., Bull. 76:307–350.
1966 (with W. G. McIntire) Australian tidal flats. La. State Univ. Press., Univ. Studies, Coastal Studies Series, 48 pp.
Smith, W. G. (see Coleman)
Steers, J. A.
1942 The coastline of England and Wales. Cambridge (Univ. Press), 547 pp.
1964 The coastline of England and Wales. Cambridge (Univ. Press), 750 pp. Reprint of the 1942 edition omitting photography and adding 13 short chapters for updating.
Strabo
Circa 7 B.C. Geography 14 . 1 . 24.
Tylor, A.
1872 On the formation of deltas, and on evidence of great changes in sea-level during the glacial period. Geol. Mag., 9:292–299.
Wright, M. (see Morgan)

4 / TROPICAL ISLAND INVESTIGATIONS

Four years of my boyhood were spent in the Hawaiian Islands. This may have some bearing on why I enjoy the climate and lush, green landscapes of Louisiana, and why since 1956 I have spent as much time as possible in the tropics. From a personal standpoint it is highly fortunate that tropical islands present so many interesting coastal problems. Some of these will be discussed here on a topical basis. In most cases the same problems are present on mainland coasts and are not wholly insular. While these investigations are not necessarily closely related to one another, each is regarded as significant in the general problem of understanding the world's sea coasts.

BEACH ROCK

My first diversion from studying mineralogical aspects of beach morphology in the Lesser Antilles occurred on the south coast of St. Lucia, where Harold Simmons and Peter H. Martin-Kaye took me to an outcrop of beach rock (Pl. 28). Although I had read about it to some extent, my interest had been indifferent. Coming into contact with a field example, however, changed my attitude completely. Beach rock was puzzling enough to become my chief research interest for about five years.

Beach rock is cemented beach material that crops out at about mean sea level in areas of small tidal range, or at about high neap-tide level if the range is large. The cemented aggregate may consist of quartz sand, black sand with high content of heavy minerals, finer-grained coastal marsh or swamp sediments, or whatever else the beach may be composed of. On the south coast of Jamaica it occurs as a coarse conglomerate. It has been reported to contain shells of World War II cartridges on some Pacific islands. At Ramie Air Force Base, northwestern Puerto Rico, it includes remnants of steel landing mats that were used by trucks in connection with mining sand. Quite commonly it preserves Indian or other artifacts, such as Coca Cola bottle caps, knives and forks, or toys used by children playing in the sand. At San Juan, Puerto Rico, it includes materials of a refuse heap and at Central Aguirre, east of Ponce, on the south coast, it contains iron shavings, nails, and even some remains of cloth. But most commonly beach rock forms in white, calcareous sand and is devoid of artifacts.

Beach rock is a distinct hazard to persons in small boats who intend to nose into a sandy beach to make a landing. As it crops out approximately at sea level in many cases it is not likely to be visible if the sea state is other than dead calm. Its front may be an intermittently submerged vertical wall as immovable and rugged as a block of concrete varying up to three or four feet in thickness. The thickness depends on fluctuations of the water table and is least where the range between high and low tide is small.

Commonly several bands of beach rock occur separated by shallow strips of water (Pl. 29). The bands may resemble pavements up to thirty feet or more wide, but ordinarily ten or less. In such cases the oldest band lies farthest seaward and the youngest continues inland, un-

PLATE 28. Beach rock on Anse Noir, south coast of St. Lucia.

PLATE 29. Parallel bands of beach rock on the retreating beach of Boca de Vieja, west of San Juan, Puerto Rico.

der the beach. Banding occurs because beach rock crops out only along retreating coasts. An inner band may be rather friable, in some cases sufficiently so that it may be crumbled in one's hand, but outer bands are tough and durable.

In cases where a retreating coast alters its configuration rapidly, remnant bands of beach rock commonly are the best evidence of earlier strandline positions. Commonly they jut out tangentially at bends. Behind them the water may be sufficiently deep to be used by small boats. Sheltered harbors lie in lee of some beach-rock bands, as near Voula, southeast of Athens, Greece. Notable changes in coastal configuration are recorded at several places around the coast of Grande Terre, Guadeloupe. A wide area of shallow bottoms north of Port Louis, on the west coast, tapers northward between the present strandline and a band of beach rock that diverges seaward from Pointe des Mangles. West of Pointe des Châteaux, at the eastern tip of the island, a complicated bit of coastal history is preserved in beach-rock bands (Pl. 30). After considerable coastal recession occurred in a small cove, some change in the vicinity brought sand to the coast in such quantity that the cove became a prograding coast and accumulated beach deposits seaward from the bands of beach rock that record the earlier history of retreat. Later, the coast again retreated, leaving a broad band of younger beach rock that truncates all older trends (Russell, 1959 and 1962; Russell and McIntire, 1965). Professor McIntire and I discovered a former connection between Flat and Gabriel islands, off the north coast of Mauritius, evidenced today by bands of beach rock jutting out from each island in the direction of the other (Pl. 31). The beach formerly connecting the islands has disappeared. In these and many other examples of changes in strandline position, the time involved at most is probably a few decades, and certainly less than a century or two. But some beach rock has survived for several millenia.

PLATE 30. Older bands of beach rock (right) on the shore of a cove are covered by a younger band (left) with a different orientation, near Pointe des Châteaux, Guadeloupe.

PLATE 31. Beach-rock bands from Flat Island once connected directly with bands extending from Gabriel Island, north of Mauritius. These were formed in a beach that once connected the two islands.

The most astonishing example of coastal retreat and beach-rock exposure with which I am familiar occurs at Cluny, on the north coast of Basse Terre, Guadeloupe. I have returned there almost yearly since 1956, to witness the exposure of beach rock at the base of a rapidly retreating sea cliff (Fig. 32). Informants described the place as having been a popular recreation beach prior to 1952, when a violent storm initiated coastal retreat and the exposure of a band of beach rock that reduced the value of the beach from the standpoint of swimming or activities associated with the presence of abundant sand. The main highway around the island, which I had used in 1956, was in part washed away and relocated in 1958. By 1959 the sea cliff had retreated locally past the former road location as shown in our instrumental sur-

Fig. 32. Surveyed record of sea-cliff retreat and beach-rock bands in 1959 at Cluny, Basse Terre, Guadeloupe, with estimated sea-cliff position in 1965. BR-1, BR-2, etc., are individual bands of beach rock exposed during coastal retreat. The road was used for automobile traffic in 1956. New beach rock is present as far inland as the 1965 sea cliff. Vertical sections A-A' and B-B' indicate the position of the water table and the lower limit of incipient beach rock in 1959, just east of the area of exposed beach rock.

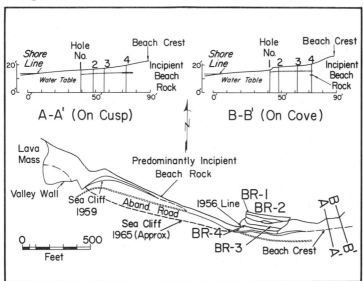

vey. It had retreated as much as 200 feet by 1965, into a coastal flat densely covered by tropical rain forest. Band after band of beach rock has become exposed along the shore. The newest bands occur in sediments that underlay forest a few years ago (Pl. 32).

Explaining the origin of beach rock was a baffling problem at first. In the West Indies I had found it on both windward and lee coasts. It occurred in a concentration of heavy-mineral black sand to the west of Arecibo, on the north coast of Puerto Rico, at Anse Noir on St. Lucia, and in various other places, yet most commonly in white, calcareous sand, and in materials of various textures ranging up to coarse conglomerates. Bands ran the length of some beaches but outcrops were small and localized in many other cases. Beaches displaying excellent examples one year might not have visible beach rock a year later. Indian artifacts of considerable antiquity were found on Cato Beach on the south coast of Grenada, yet beach rock appearing equally well devel-

PLATE 32. Water-table rock exposed as the low sea cliff at Cluny, Guadeloupe, retreats rapidly changes into typical beach rock, shown in the foreground.

oped, on the basis of durability and induration, commonly contains artifacts that are but a few years old.

Noting that beach rock is likely to be covered by algae or algal crusts, my first inclination was to regard the cementation as of algal origin. For that reason, in 1958, I took two physiological algologists, Professor Robert Krauss and his assistant, Raymond Galloway, of the University of Maryland, to more than eighty beaches on islands extending from Puerto Rico to Grenada in the belief that they could explain the cementation process. This was a most fortunate investigation, mainly because it eliminated algae from the problem and focused attention on ground-water relationships (Krauss and Galloway, 1960). We found that all beach-rock localities occur in connection with coastal recession and that outcrops are displayed because beach sediments were removed above the level of the water table.

In 1959, I took Professors Frank Germano and Alva Lowman, of the department of Civil Engineering, Louisiana State University, to many beaches in the same area to map beach-rock outcrops and to establish precisely their relationships to the water table. Most of the information shown in Figure 32 was mapped during that trip. Other maps and sections were published in my 1962 paper. The switch from algologists to engineers as field associates indicated that considerable progress had occurred in solving the problem of beach-rock origin.

Professor McIntire, in 1960 and 1961, established the fact that water-table cementation extends continuously from exposures of beach rock inland for at least 1,600 feet on Mauritius (Fig. 33) (McIntire, 1961; Russell and McIntire, 1965). On Viti Levu, Fiji, and on the coast of Queensland, in 1963, he and I referred to inland outcrops of the cemented layer as "stream rock" because we found it along the banks of streams (Pl. 33). This designation is exactly as logical as "beach rock," but we now regret introducing the term into the literature in 1965, because

PLATE 33. The platform upon which the automobile stands is the surface of stream rock exposed in the foreground, Beautiful Pool, near Port Hedland, Western Australia.

Fig. 33. Mauritius, showing beach rock localities and sections surveyed across quarry floors. Radiocarbon dates on corals in water-table rock suggest that sea level has remained essentially in its present position during the last 3,925 years but in part the impression would be corrected were a larger scale used for the sections. Localities with oldest dates in actuality were slightly lower than younger dated samples closer to the shore. A stream rock locality is indicated on Black River (slightly modified, after McIntire).

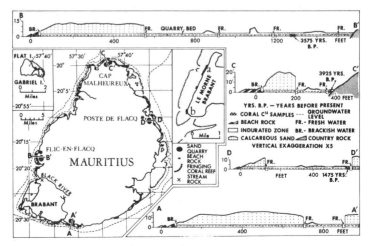

during the following Antillean investigations we found
an equivalent layer around a lagoon north of Port Louis,
Guadaloupe, and do not care to confuse matters by call-
ing it "lagoon rock." A more appropriate terminology
would be to regard the entire genus as "water-table
rock," and to recognize outcrop locations as species.
Even the specific term "beach rock" is unfortunate because the beach plays only a passive role in its origin.

One of the puzzling questions that arose early in
beach-rock studies was determining the source of the
calcium carbonate that cements its constituent particles.
Limestone hinterland appeared to be favorable but not
necessary because beach rock occurs in pocket beaches
on Oahu, Basse Terre, Mauritius, and other volcanic
islands. The Atlantic coast of Puerto Rico, much of which
has a limestone hinterland, exhibits many long and excellent beach-rock exposures, but other coasts of that
island exhibit few or none. Streams reaching them cross
relatively little limestone, and beach sands are typically
black and iron-rich, rather than calcareous. At Barriada
Linboglia, on the south coast, the calcium carbonate content of water in a tiny stream leading to a small outcrop
of beach rock was but 4 parts per million, whereas in
water collected just offshore it was 480. The total chlo-
rides in the stream were but 177 ppm, whereas in adjacent sea water they amounted to 20,384. Comparisons
of this kind suggest that the lime cement comes from sea
water, but this is not the case. The calcium carbonate
ordinarily is supplied by ground water or comes from
beach sand. The pocket beaches with beach rock on volcanic islands invariably consist of almost pure concen-
trations of coral fragments, echinoid spines, foraminifera, *Halimeda* flakes, or other calcareous organic materials. The source of lime is the beach itself.

When examined under a binocular microscope calcareous fragments in beach sand above the water table are
ordinarily smooth and display polished surfaces (Pl. 34).

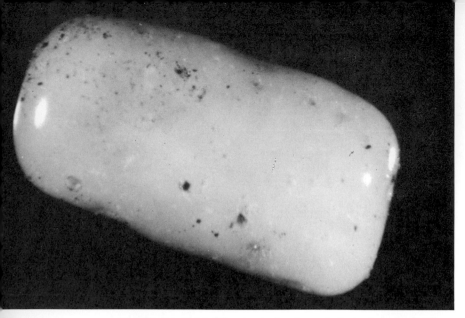

PLATE 34. Echinoid spine in beach sand above the water table is smoothly polished (length of spine about 1 mm).

PLATE 35. Echinoid spine in beach sand below the water table has undergone pitting and losses by solution (length of spine about 1 mm).

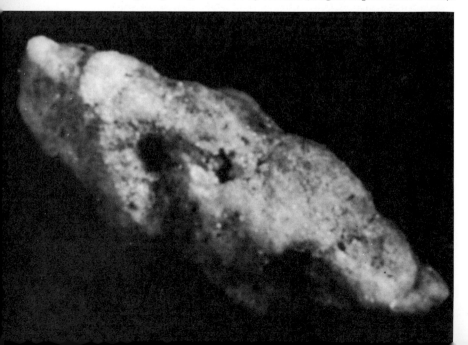

This condition is explained by abrasion occurring as the grains are moved about under the force of wave impacts of intensity sufficient to cause surficial changes in beach topography, or by currents within the swash zone and for some distance seaward across the lower beach. These are the grains commonly in contact with sea water and they are free of any depositional coating of lime.

On the other hand, calcareous fragments below the water table are typically leached irregularly and display pitting that results from solution in groundwater (Pl. 35). This water is much less saline than sea water. It freshens in amazingly short distances inland across most beaches. From a limestone hinterland the water may be disagreeably hard, but in areas of moderate or heavy rainfall it is commonly more or less potable toward the inner side of a beach.

Within the zone of water-table fluctuations, sand, rock, or organic fragments display dull, irregular coatings of lime (Pl. 36). The upper boundary of cementation is not sharp as a rule because it rises along plant roots and displays other irregularities associated with variations in permeability (Pl. 37). The groundwater is likely to be so heavily charged with calcium carbonate that it appears milky and if one plunges his arm into it his skin becomes covered by innumerable small flakes of lime that are difficult to remove (Pl. 38). The local environment is one in which cementation of grains takes place rapidly.

Examination of beach rock in thin sections under a petrographic microscope reveals the sequence in which cementation takes place. Initially a thin coating of calcite surrounds each grain, leaving as voids most of the spaces between grains (Pl. 39). In this initial stage of cementation the beach rock is readily crushed by squeezing in one's hand. As cementation progresses the coatings thicken at the expense of voids and the beach rock becomes better indurated. At length, nearly all voids are

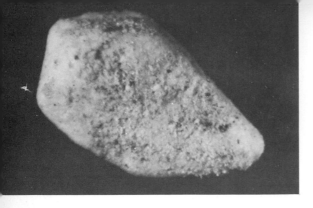

PLATE 36. Sand grain in the water-table zone of a beach has acquired a rough, calcareous coating (grain about 0.8 mm long).

PLATE 37. While cementation along the zone of water-table fluctuation below the spade is general, lime deposits occur up the small tree trunk to a considerably higher level. Nearly all the wood had decayed so the roots and trunk are essentially hollow lime tubes. Located in the quarry at Flic-en-Flacq, Mauritius (Fig. 33, west end of quarry bed on section B-B').

PLATE 38. Milky groundwater in the hole below the pick was fairly potable, 1 km west of Moule, Guadeloupe. Six inches of incipient beach rock above occurs in the zone of water-table fluctuation.

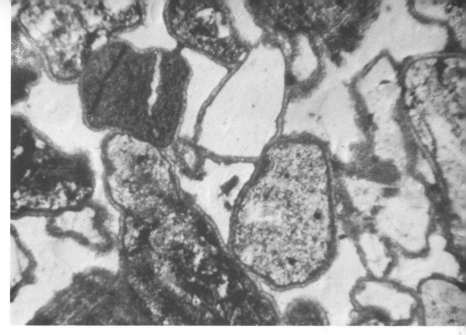

PLATE 39. *(Above)* In this incipient beach rock each mineral grain, rock fragment, or organic particle is surrounded by a thin calcite coating that appears dark in comparison with open spaces—voids—between grains (width shown is slightly more than 1 mm).

PLATE 40. *(Below)* Rock and organic fragments in well-indurated beach rock are surrounded by rims of calcite that appear white in comparison with the calcareous cement that has filled most voids. An open void remains near the center and others toward the bottom of the photomicrograph, which is slightly more than 1 mm wide.

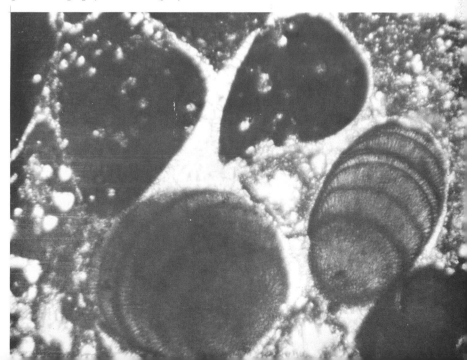

filled and the beach rock resembles physically a mass of concrete (Pl. 40). The filling normally occurs in two stages, the first of which is characterized by increasing thickness of the early grain coatings, and the second of cement that completes void filling. The earlier cementation is by relatively pure, colorless calcite, while the later and final cementation is somewhat brownish, iron-stained calcite, of much finer texture.

At Cluny, Basse Terre, where we have watched the process on repeated occasions, we find that newly exposed "water-table rock" is characterized by initial stages of cementation. After a season or two of exposure to the atmosphere, spray of sea water, and occasional overwash by waves, the second phase of cementation occurs and the rock becomes hard and durable. The initial cementation appears to occur in an environment of stagnant or sluggish flow of ground water, while the second takes place after the circulation is more active. Further observations are necessary before our understanding of the process is complete. That the cementation is not uniquely associated with sea water is demonstrated by the fact that exactly similar changes occur in water-table rock exposed along stream banks located well inland, as at Half Tide, south of Mackay, Queensland; Bluewater Creek, north of Townsville, Queensland; and along many other creeks and rivers.

In several reports we referred to newly exposed water-table rock as "incipient beach rock." Where the water table is relatively flat and the slope of the beach very gentle, at times of moderate wave energy considerable areas of this rock may be exposed. In one case, in the Five Islands district of Antigua, I studied an extensive exposure in considerable detail, with the intent of returning in subsequent years to witness steps in its conversion to typical beach rock (Pl. 41). But six months later the whole outcrop, as well as incipient beach rock extending back some distance under the beach, had been

PLATE 41. Newly exposed incipient beach rock, on a beach in the Five Islands district of Antigua.

removed by high-energy waves during one or more storms. Since then the beach volume and width have increased at times along this beach, covering beach rock that was observed on earlier trips and initiating new cementation of sand in the vicinity of the water table.

Extremely puzzling for several years was the presence of beach rock on some beaches, its absence from others, and its occurrence in very restricted parts of many beaches. Early in our investigations we found that beach rock does not occur on regularly prograding beaches. They widen too rapidly to permit exposure of incipient beach rock and its cementation into durable bands. Later, we found that on parts of beaches regularly subjected to progradation and recession, the incipient beach rock is commonly attacked by waves with sufficient energy to break the bonds of cementation and leave uncemented sand as a residue. Around the almost circular refraction bay of Anabyssos, toward the end of the peninsula leading to Sunion, southeast of Athens, Greece, the only place that beach rock is exposed is directly across the bay from its narrow opening into the Saronic Gulf. This appears to be the only localized area of beach retreat. On most cove beaches the central part of the beach is much better exposed to high-energy waves so that incipient beach rock is frequently washed away, and when wave energy drops, prograding occurs, so permanent beach rock is unable to form, whereas on one or both sides, where storm waves strike with less vigor, the attack is not so extreme, variations in exposed sand volumes are minor, and beach rock is more likely to become firmly cemented and survive.

The dip of stratification of beach sand is normally a few degrees greater than the slope of the water table. For that reason beach rock bands have more gentle seaward slope than dips in sand deposits. If several pavements are present, each represents a time during which sufficient cementation occurred to insure survival even though exposure to considerable wave energy occurred later on. The troughs of water between bands date from occasions when wave energy was high enough to remove sand to the rear of a beach-rock band, together with a strip of incipient beach rock below the removed beach sand. The next pavement developed its induration later on and survived because some period of relative tranquility permitted its cementation.

The arrangment of beach-rock bands commonly appears to violate principles of stratification in most sedimentary rocks, as should be the case, because beach rock occurs along the water table, rather than as stratified layers in a sedimentary deposit. Younger bands of beach rock appear to be dipping beneath older bands, but this actually is not the case. When formed, each band ended in a trough of water on its seaward side, so there is no overlapping as in the case of tiles or shingles on a roof. When an individual band is examined, in most cases it evidences stratification exactly like that of the beach in which it originated and may display cross-bedding or other depositional structures. On a microtopographic scale more resistant layers lead upward into cuestalike ridges separated by valleys along less-resistant layers. This is true shinglelike structure associated with stratification, but not with cementation, which is more horizontal in orientation.

As a beach retreats landward the entire groundwater system is modified and the level of the water table is lowered at any specific place. The seaward level is essentially that of the sea on Caribbean islands, where the tidal range is low, or the water table emerges along a spring line at about high neap-tide level on coasts where the range is high. If considerable retreat has taken place, say half a mile, the water table along the present strandline is probably several feet lower than was the case before the retreat started. Cementation likely occurred at several levels, each representing a period of relative inactivity, first at some higher level, then at successively lower levels. During times of violent storms, sand may be removed at high elevations along a beach and some of the water-table rock cemented when the beach extended farther seaward may become exposed for the first time. An example of this occurs east of Beautiful Pool, some five miles east of Port Hedland, Western Australia. Beach rock that appears to be abnormally high on the upper beach owes its position to its having been cemented many decades ago, although only recently exposed to the atmosphere.

Many anomalous occurrences of beach rock result from the fact that the sand underlying it is not as firmly cemented as that along the water table. Waves commonly undermine beach-rock pavements. In many cases isolated slabs of considerable area slip seaward, attain atypical slopes, and arrive at positions well below the levels where they formed. In some cases the pavements hold together reasonably well but settle in complex ways because their foundational support has been removed irregularly. Near the Fannie Bay Hotel, Darwin, Northern Territory, Australia, there has been considerable distortion and modification of beach rock. In places it slopes landward and over a wide area; it also exhibits many little anticlines, synclines, and other geologic structures on a small scale. The whole outcrop is also complicated by the fact that detached slabs have been carried landward by high waves to settle on other beach-rock outcrops, to which they have become firmly cemented. The most complicated deformation of beach rock that I have observed occur at Lykouriza, some 39 km southeast of Athens. Collapse has resulted in a variety of fractures, structures such as plunging anticlines or synclines, and the detachment of large slabs, some of which have been overturned and cemented to underlying beach rock. The area of complex distortion is about 150 m in length and in places more than 20 m wide.

In some cases beach rock is useful for determining changes in level between land and sea. At Campos, Ikaria Island, near the coast of Turkey, beach rock submerged to a depth of six feet or so occurs at the level of a village that is now buried under coarse gravels near the mouth of a valley. The method used for the construction of the buried buildings is said to be that of 3,000 years ago. As there are many earthquakes on the island and evidences of active faulting are numerous, it may be presumed that the old settlement, together with the beach, has been faulted down to its present position. There is ample evidence that the level of the Mediterranean has not risen several feet during the time interval involved. To the west of Cerro Gordo, on the north coast of Puerto Rico, beach rock crops out on a Pleistocene terrace about twenty feet above sea level. The rock has abrasional flutings resembling those common on beach rock today that is subject to abrasion and solution associated with wave action. Long bands of Pleistocene

PLATE 42. Pleistocene beach rock overlies reef-flat deposits near Cape Cuvier, Western Australia, north of Carnarvon. These formations are differentially warped but in most places indicate a late Pleistocene sea level of about 20 feet higher than that today.

beach rock occur along the coast of Western Australia, north of Cape Cuvier (Pl. 42). These indicate a sea level about twenty feet above that at present and are associated with Pleistocene beach sands extending ten or more feet higher, just as is the case of Recent sands along today's beaches in the vicinity (Fig. 27).

Utmost caution, however, should be exhibited in relating beach-rock elevation to minor changes of level, such as five feet or less. On Cocos-Keeling, Indian Ocean, shoreline configuration is changing rapidly and beach rock up to an elevation of eight feet or so apparently formed not many years ago when the water table locally stood considerably higher than it does now, after considerable sea-cliff retreat. The latest layer of beach rock is being formed close to sea level on the inner side of a wide reef flat. Other atolls may be suspect of having had similar history. Many of them exhibit retreating sea cliffs.

QUATERNARY SEA LEVELS

West of Rio Bueno, on the north coast of Jamaica, starting a mile from the town, in 1964 I found complete evidence of a higher stand of a Quaternary sea. A notch up
to about six feet deep and ten feet high was eroded into
country rock consisting of massive limestone (Pl. 43).
What made the find exciting was the presence of numerous mollusk borings, with shells intact, low in the notch,

PLATE 43. Pleistocene sea level of 20 feet is indicated in this notch,
1 mile west of Rio Bueno, Jamaica. The party is collecting mollusk
shells in their *in situ* borings above many small coral heads.

and below them a number of *in situ* coral heads in growth position, duplicating exactly those living nearby at about low-tide level (Pl. 44). The mollusk borings had a vertical range of about four feet. Shells within them were "dead" from the standpoint of radiocarbon dating. Remnant beach deposits in the vicinity contained a rich fauna similar to that now living along the coast. Using convenient bench marks we surveyed the elevation of this old sea stand and found that it approximated twenty feet (Fig. 34). This agreed with the difference in level between fossil and living coral heads. Seaward from the notch a fossil reef flat about a quarter of a mile wide displays a fauna of beautifully preserved corals and other organisms that, according to Dr. Tom Goreau, a member of our party and coral specialist at the University of the West Indies, display exactly the same ecological associations as those along the coast today. In 1965, Dr. McIntire, found a similar notch at the same elevation on Cayman Brac.

What amazed us most about the Rio Bueno notch was its occurrence at the same level as one of the major stands of Quaternary sea level on coasts of the Indian Ocean. We had excellent reasons for believing that parts of the coast of Western Australia and of the crystalline-rock islands of Seychelles are stable areas with regard to Quaternary crustal movements, but did not regard the West Indies as exhibiting stability extending back into the Pleistocene. But later on, we found that this is the case on at least several islands in the arcs of the Lesser Antilles, as mentioned in the last chapter.

One of the most interesting discoveries made by McIntire and me in 1964 was a Pleistocene sea cliff facing in a diametrically opposite direction from that of an active Recent cliff in its immediate vicinity at Pointe des Châteaux, the extreme eastern tip of Grande Terre, Guadeloupe (Fig. 35). The summit of the point stands at an elevation of 141 feet, capping a nearly vertical cliff

PLATE 44. Mollusk borings in Rio Bueno notch, Jamaica.

Fig. 34. Sea-level relationship between features along the latest
Pleistocene and Recent high stands on the north coast of Jamaica, near
Rio Bueno.

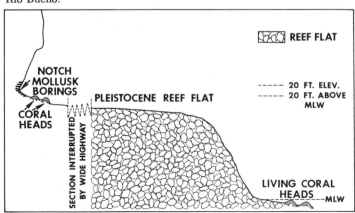

that is under rapid retreat because it faces directly all trade-wind and other Atlantic waves arriving from the east. There are small embayments along this cliff and in one near the point a Pleistocene sea cliff is exposed that faces westward. The Recent cliff and its embayments are being driven back into the remnant of what not long ago was a much higher hill, as judged from its steep westward backslope and knife-edge summit. A great deal of colluvial debris covers the remnant hill. At the base of the fossil sea cliff is a remnant beach at an elevation somewhat above 20 feet. Both the old cliff and beach are duplicated in another exposure on a lower hill to the north of the main point. A discovery of reversal in direction between a Pleistocene and a Recent sea cliff is interesting, but the really impressive thing in the vicinity is the presence of a reef flat around the shores of Anse des Châteaux, west of the fossil sea cliff. It stands at 20 feet. The Pleistocene sea cliff was cut by waves advancing across the Anse, from the northwest. Within that old bay there was an island that now stands as a low hill, Mourne Petite Saline. On the shores of the island beaches developed which retain a complete transition between reef-flat and beach deposits. Fragments of coral, conchs and many other kinds of shells, as well as typical beach sediments and debris rise to an elevation of 25 feet around the old island. Many of the conchs are entire, in-

Fig. 35. While the active sea cliff at Pointe des Châteaux, Grande Terre, Guadeloupe, faces east, the latest Pleistocene cliff faces west and was associated with beaches and a reef flat indicating a 20-foot stand of sea level.

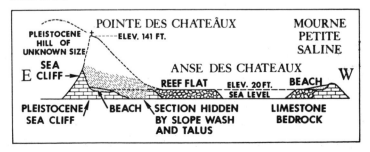

dicating that they had not been collected by man as food. Conchs dating from pre-European times exhibit circular borings made for the purpose of cutting the edible muscle from the shell. Those of more recent times display jagged holes, resulting from the use of steel or iron implements as punches.

A general rule useful when searching for Quaternary sea stands is to pay particular attention to windward coasts of trade-wind islands. Along these east coasts we find the most flourishing reefs and best developed reef flats today, and this was also the case in the past. Almost the whole east coast of Barbuda displays a reef-flat bench at an elevation of twenty feet. The best evidence of higher sea stands on Antigua, as far as we know, occurs on Soldier Point, one of the southeast tips of the island. On Grenada the best locality is probably on the east side of Point Laurant, near the north end of the island, to the west of Sauteurs. But other headlands are not to be dismissed. On Puerto Rico, a road excavation near Punta Higuero, the westernmost tip of the island, cut through concealing colluvial float into an excellent reef-flat remnant at an elevation of thirty feet, and other informative localities indicating that older stand of sea level occur along the Atlantic coast east of Punta Chivato, and on Punta Salines. We also found the thirty-foot level at several places on Guadeloupe.

ALGAL FLATS

Beach-rock investigations led us directly into a decidedly more baffling problem. On the seaward side of beach-rock exposures and particularly in cases where several more or less parallel bands are present, commonly there is a reefal accumulation of organic deposits on surfaces exposed most directly to wave action (Fig. 36). The accumulation is predominantly algal and calcareous. More or less massive single benches may cover the beach rock

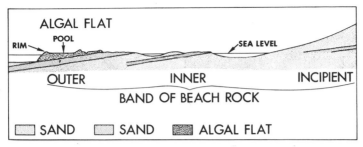

Fig. 36. Relationship of many algal flats to bands of beach rock.

or a series of little flats that form terracettes separated by distinct rims (Pl. 45). These occur not only on beach rock but also on dune rock (eolianite) and in many other situations. In more massive examples we find complex assemblages of algae and animals in considerable variety. We have collected many samples, both with and without living organisms, and have studied the flats with considerable care, but as yet have not reached definite conclusions as to their origin. We are inclined to believe that we are dealing with several distinctly different features, unified superficially by similarities in location and ap-

PLATE 45. Pools on algal flat, near Chalky Mount, Barbados.

pearance. At any rate, we intend to pursue the problem and will not feel content until we arrive at a much better understanding of its ramifications.

Many observers have concluded that the flats are purely erosional in origin (Wentworth, 1939) and we agree that this is the case in some instances, as at various places around Rottnest Island, west of Perth, Western Australia. But most examples are surfaces of organic accumulations that cover beach rock or other types of country rock, where absolute disproof of erosional origin is evident. One explanation that has gained several adherents considers the flats as erosional, but that their levels are conditioned by protective organic growths. Kaye, who prefers the term "tidal terrace" to the nomenclature of other writers, regards conspicuous benches along the Atlantic coast of Puerto Rico as the product of differential erosion in which the eolianite both above and below the flats has been removed, while protective algae, and in rare cases other organisms, have preserved the country rock by covering it in the intertidal zone (Kaye, 1959).

Proximity to the intertidal zone, together with a higher strip subject to frequent contact with waves, is certainly a characteristic of features we have described as *algal flats*. From personal observation and opinions of informants, I gain the impression that if desiccated more than fours hours most of the biota present would fail to survive. As on active reef crests, life flourishes most vigorously where wave impacts are most severe and frequent. For that reason algal flats commonly attain highest elevation on headlands and slope to lower levels in embayments. The lowest level they attain, as far as I have observed, is close to high neap-tide level.

In examples where algal flats display conspicuous terracettes the highest pools occur where most vigorous breakers strike and, together with all other pools in the system, have rims that rise to a level that permits surplus water to flow gradually from one level to the next, down to one or more outlet channels through which it returns to the sea (Pl. 46). All pools are kept filled and their plant and animal inhabitants—small fish, sea cucumbers, echinoids, gastropods, algae, and other organisms—thrive. This generalization holds true whether the algal flats occur along narrow benches fronting sea cliffs or lie between coral-reef crests and a shore several hundred yards away, as at Tangangge on the south coast of Viti Levu, Fiji. Where the width is narrow, as on a sea cliff, the highest pool ordinarily lies innermost and lower pools form steps seaward. But if the terracette system is wide, as near Contrabandiers, southwest of Rabat, Morocco (Pl. 47), or where the flats lie behind reefs some distance from the shore, as in many examples in the Pacific and Indian oceans, the highest pool lies farthest seaward and the return channel is located close to the shore, eventually breaking out to the sea around the end of the flat.

Thus far, our petrographic studies are not confirming field observations suggesting that thin algal crusts protect underlying rock from erosion. What appear to be

PLATE 46. Terracettes on algal flat that developed around an eolianite island, near Palmas Atlas, Puerto Rico.

PLATE 47. Terracettes on algal flat developed on the side of an outcrop of eroded eolianite. The pools descend progressively from the Atlantic Ocean toward the beach at Contrabandiers, near Rabat, Morocco.

PLATE 48. Thick algal flat that has grown out from eolianite country rock, 12.8 km west of Palmas Atlas, Puerto Rico.

crusts in the field ordinarily turn out to be nothing more than case-hardened, oxidized alteration of algal debris, associated oolite, and included remains of mollusks and other organisms. We thought we had an excellent example of thin crusts near Port Hedland, Western Australia, covering both rims and pool floors. Our collections included specimens that exhibited both the presumed crusts and material beneath. In thin sections we found that the crusts are superficial alteration products and that the unaltered rock is exactly that in the crusts, not the basement rock; eolianite, which crops out in the vicinity of the pools.

In the West Indies we find that on benches where undermining and frequent detachment of slabs of rock result from severe wave impact, the benches are narrow and only thinly covered by algal or other organisms. But on stable benches that have become wide the organic layer may be several feet thick and is certainly a depositional feature (Pl. 48).

These conclusions are somewhat tentative. We have considerable more field work and sampling to do before we feel that our results are thoroughly demonstrated, or found to be faulty.

REEFS AND REEF FLATS

Although the terminology is somewhat confused and some may disagree, it is probably most useful to regard as *coral reef* such calcareous deposits as exhibit corals and other organisms in essentially the same relative positions as they occupied while alive, and a *reef flat* as a clastic deposit dominated by fragmental reef debris in more or less random orientations (Pl. 49). A reef flat ordinarily accumulates landward from an active reef. The front of an active reef is a foreslope alive with living things down to a depth of ten fathoms or so, below which it may terminate in a sand deposit and become less interesting biologically. The crest of a reef and its foreslope teem with life, both sessile and free moving. This is also

PLATE 49. Typical Pleistocene reef flat with blocks of coral and other clastic debris in random orientations secondarily cemented into a durable mass, 9.3 km west of Palmas Atlas, Puerto Rico.

PLATE 50. Reef in the far distance is marked by a line of breakers. Behind it is the lagoon, much of which displays reef flat at low tide. In the foreground are blocks of coral that have been transported landward to become part of the beach, West Island, Cocos-Keeling.

true of isolated *patch reefs that* rise, here and there, from shallow bottoms. Reefs enlarge by seaward growth, but are unable to rise appreciably above the level of low tide. The transition from reef to reef flat may be gradual. A reef ordinarily becomes established some distance offshore, isolating water landward as a lagoon (Pl. 50). The reef grows outward rather than landward and as it does so its active front supplies blocks that become detached and when high waves are present, to be transported over the crest to settle in the lagoon or on other similar debris, building a reef flat. The reef flat is commonly highest near the reef crest and the deepest parts of the lagoon occur toward the shore, where the supply of reefal debris is diminished. But conversion of the lagoon into a reef flat takes place for other reasons as well. Algae and a great variety of animals flourish in the lagoon and their deposits or remains settle there, decreasing the water volume (Pl. 51). Among the animals present in West Indian lagoons colonies of staghorn corals are likely to be numerous and their debris bulks heavy in fill material, as do their smaller fragments as constituents of beaches along the shore. The initial biota of the lagoon floor is one that grows in water considerably deeper than that toward the reef crest, where elkhorn corals and other shallow-water forms of life predominate (Pl. 52). As the lagoon shoals, organisms requiring more sheltered environments, including those provided by shallow pools, become larger parts of the assemblage of living things.

What many people, unversed in biology, are likely to regard as specimens of coral are parts of colonial structures; lime secreted to provide stability necessary for the growth of individual polyps, which ordinarily are very small. The habit of a colonial structure depends on its location. Down a reef front most corals tend to build tabular structures that project forward about horizontally. The same species of polyps may build a thin encrusting layer on the shore side of a reef crest. Thus mor-

PLATE 51. Flourishing life on a lagoon floor, Grand Cayman Island. Staghorn coral colonies are consipicuous in the foreground as rodlike stalks. These are brittle and are readily reduced to fragments. Photograph by Norwood Rector.

PLATE 52. Massive elkhorn coral colonies in shallow water, Grand Cayman Island. The upper surface of the coral deposit is relatively flat and within about three feet of the water surface, which dominates the upper half of the picture, where shadows are cast by waves. Photograph by Norwood Rector.

phological variations in habit become confusing to the layman. He doubts that a massive coral in one place is the same species as an encrusting form somewhere else. But the taxonomist looks at the organism itself, not its colonial secretion. Possibly even more confusing to a layman is the terrific variety of appearances exhibited by sponges, some of which are familiar to him but others appear as thin gelatinous films coating whatever substrate they are attached to, even a small shell. While it is not appropriate to refer to these animals as being vicious, some of them are the greatest enemies of corals, covering them, thriving on the lime of the colony, and completely smothering the coral polyps below them. Across lagoons and in many other situations it may be observed that many or most of the coral colonies are dead because sponges have killed all living polyps. The colonies disintegrate rather rapidly after being killed, breaking into the fragments, including coral sand, that floor lagoon bottoms in many places or that become concentrated along beaches.

The buttresses and grooves that characterize reef fronts are the most perfect mechanisms known for dampening wave energy (Munk and Sargent, 1948). As a wave dashes into a reef most of its energy is dissipated because it entrains considerable air while breaking and is turned into extraordinarily complex systems of turbulent flow. It is exhilarating to stand on a reef crest and watch nearby waves, possibly ten feet high, rushing toward you every few seconds, in perfect confidence that at most the surge will be only from ankle to knee deep after most of the initial wave energy is expended and tranquil flow washes over onto the reef flat. Buttresses and grooves occur in patterns determined by the environment of wave attack. Were the energy reduced the grooves would fill with organic growth to some extent and the reef front would become smoother. As the reef grows seaward, the pattern for any particular place remains about the same,

PLATE 53. A deep surge channel leads across the crest of the reef, West Island, Cocos-Keeling. Flow is violent in the channel and its direction alternates according to arrivals of wave crests and troughs.

in so far as shape and energy characteristics are concerned.

A part of the wave-dampening system are surge channels of considerable depth that are eroded back through the reef crest for various distances into reef-flat materials (Pl. 53). One stands on the side of a surge channel in awe to watch currents that sweep violently to and fro as wave crests and troughs alternately impinge on the reef. Except under conditions of very low sea state, a person who inadvertently falls or is swept into a surge channel ordinarily has little chance of survival. On the reef along the seaward side of West Island, Cocos-Keeling, bodies are ordinarily recovered west of the most conspicuous reef, as they are being washed back toward a beach. No native would consider recovering them along the reef front. The favorable conditions for line fishing often tempt persons to approach the banks of surge channels too closely.

In cases where a wide reef flat has developed and most of the area between reef crest and the shore stands close to low-tide level, algal flats are likely to develop. Those along the south coast of Viti Levu have pools floored with mud because they are densely inhabited by sea cucumbers, which have ravenous appetites for microorganisms in mud, which they work and rework with vigor, reducing all mineral particles to extremely small size. Starfish, brittlestars, jelly fish, and a variety of other animals form colorful assemblages in these pools.

Coral reefs touch or closely approach the shore at various points on islands and headlands along a coast (Pl. 54). Normally they exhibit gaps out from river mouths. These are commonly regarded as being caused by turbid water coming from the land but probably another factor has much influence in their origin—the presence of deep submarine channels that were cut during low stands of Pleistocene sea level. On the windward coast of Mauritius the reef is very continuous and for a long distance stands well out from the shore. Although the lagoon is entered by many turbid streams with considerable discharge the only gap sufficiently deep for navigation by ships of fair size occurs toward the south, in the vicinity of Lighthouse Island. From this gap we sounded a deep, winding channel across the shallow lagoon, back toward Vieux Grand Port, the original Dutch settlement on the

PLATE 54. The reef is located along the belt in which waves break between Isle de la Passe and Lighthouse Island, Mauritius. The reef flat extends toward the left as a shoal area, beyond which there is a wide lagoon extending to the coast where Mahebourg and other towns are located.

island, not far from Mahebourg. This channel is certainly relict from the time when Rivers Champagne, des Creoles, la Chaux, and other streams joined to create a master stream leading to a sea level much lower than that today. Minor breaks in the reef occur northward, among which the most conspicuous is associated with Grand River South East.

As the level of a reef flat so broadly approximates that of low tide, the flats are extremely useful in determining Quaternary high-stands of sea level. But reefs are confined to tropical seas and are not well developed in the Atlantic, except on shores of the Gulf of Mexico and the Caribbean, and to some extent along the coast of Brazil. Even though reef flats fail to reach the shore, an excellent datum exists close to sea cliffs because small coral heads grow up to about low-tide level if there is a rocky foundation for their attachment. In cooler parts of the world eustatic sea level stands may be based somewhat less certainly on elevations of marsh deposits, which approximate the level of high tide. Although there is satisfaction in running a line of levels from some bench mark, I personally would not search very far for one nor bemoan its absence if I had some Quaternary level that exhibits features duplicated in the vicinity by Recent equivalents. The values needed for geometric eustatic conclusions are relative, not absolute. On most coasts the assumption is justified that the tidal range during higher stands of Quaternary seas was similar to that of today.

Some reefs or cays that stand well out from the shore in tropical areas pose a baffling problem if they support mangroves. Excellent examples occur east of Cabo Rojo, the southwestern tip of Puerto Rico, where mangroves grow far from land and certainly beyond limits of the island's groundwater supply. Here it is easy to become convinced that fresh water, other than rain falling locally, is unnecessary for mangrove growth. But most mangroves grow along the sides of estuaries or other

PLATE 55. Water table about a foot deep in *Halimeda* sand on a tiny cay about 5 miles from the nearest coast of Puerto Rico, east of Cabo Rojo. The water was fairly potable. Young mangroves are becoming established on the cay.

coastal indentations where considerable fresh water is present. On Trinidad one may well become convinced that fresh water is essential. The Great Mangrove Swamp at the western end of the central plain has been wasting away during the last decade or so, and the reason appears to be diversion of water from landward sources for the purpose of irrigating rice. As the area covered by rice fields has expanded, the mangroves downslope have become less vigorous. This whole question is one deserving much study. Even on Puerto Rican cays, however, there is a small local supply of fresh water where sand is present. We have found fairly potable water at a depth of about a foot in *Halimeda* sand (Pl. 55). Should a person find himself stranded on a small coral cay he may find, within short digging distance, enough fresh water to sustain him for a number of days. This is "blister water" derived from rain and it floats upon more saline water at depth. Water also occurs on long sand spits, where most people would never think of looking for it.

CORAL CAP OF BARBADOS

Barbados lies out in the Atlantic Ocean and geologically is not a member of either the arc of the "Limestone Caribbees" nor of the younger "Volcanic Caribbees," of the Lesser Antilles. William Morris Davis always referred to it as "the aberrant island of Barbados" (Davis, 1938). Its inhabitants, however, do everything possible to foster Caribbean identification as it has much tourist appeal. According to local terminology one leaves the airport near Bridgetown and flies west across the "Caribbean Sea" only to arrive on the Atlantic coast of Grenada, St. Vincent, or St. Lucia. This brings to mind a similar confusion in the southern hemisphere where one leaves a

Fig. 37. Antillean island arcs and the geological trend leading toward Barbados.

New Zealand airport to cross the Tasman Sea in order to arrive on the Pacific coast of Australia. But there, the intent of New Zealanders is to avoid any implication of close association with the nearby continent.

The Limestone "Caribbees," or Antilles, begin at Sombrero and for a short distance exhibit a trend similar to that of the Greater Antilles, but the arc swings through Anguilla, Barbuda, Antigua, Grand Terre, and ends in the southeastern part of Martinique (Fig. 37) (Schuchert, 1935). Most islands along this arc display stratified rock of Miocene or earlier age. A short distance to the west, the Volcanic "Caribbees" extend from Saba to Grenada. These islands are higher and far more picturesque because they are young and exhibit either active or dormant volcanoes. Barbados, in contrast, geologically is the

Fig. 38. Boundary between the older bedrock of the Scotland District of Barbados and the coral cap to its west and south (scarps on the coral cap, after Price).

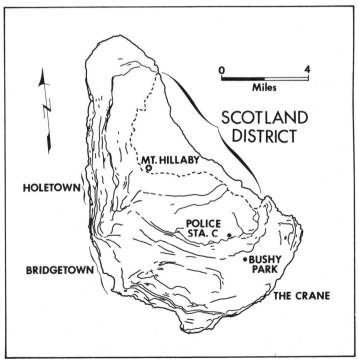

easternmost extension of an arc leading from Venezuela; a continuation of rocks and structural trends that cross the Northern Range of Trinidad and the nearby island of Tobago. The gap between there and Barbados is about 140 miles.

The Scotland District of Barbados and a strip along the east coast to the south (Fig. 38) is a museum of deformed rocks. Earliest Tertiary sediments, behaving as plastic materials, have become highly contorted. These Scotland Series beds exhibit isoclinal folding, overturning, complex faulting, and about every other known kind of structural deformation (Fig. 39). Above them lie the uplifted but relatively undeformed Oceanic Series rocks. Formerly these were regarded as of latest Tertiary age, but more recently have been assigned to a place somewhat lower in the geologic column, probably lower Miocene or even Eocene. Oceanic Series rocks were cited for many years as having originated as deposits that accumulated on the floor of the Atlantic at abyssal depth, but more recent studies of their microfauna suggests that the depth was about 1,500 feet, or possibly somewhat less. The Scotland Series rocks accumulated and had become highly deformed before the Oceanic Series was deposited-

Fig. 39. Section ENE from Holetown across the highest summit on Barbados, showing relationships between the older Tertiary (Scotland Series) and somewhat younger beds (Oceanic Series). Quaternary coral-cap rocks cover the Oceanic Series rocks toward the west.

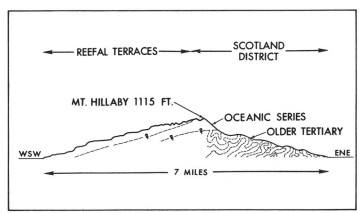

ited. After these events Barbados was elevated without much additional deformation.

Our interest in Barbados lies not in this geologic history but rather with subsequent events. The Oceanic Series is covered by a coral cap that extends over most of the island. McIntire and I examined the coral cap on a reconnaissance basis during the fall of 1964 in order to determine whether ecological observations we had been making in Caribbean coral reef areas might be useful in explaining facies contrasts within coastal-limestone rock.

The maximum elevation of the coral cap is slightly more than 1,000 feet. The highest point on the island, Mt. Hillaby, rises to 1,115 feet, with Oceanic Series rocks at its summit. The coral cap is extremely recent in age, possibly not more than a few tens of thousands of years. Many people have studied its rich fauna and all apparently agree that every species it contains is living today in the vicinity. Although we found evidences of Pleistocene changes of level on every other West Indian island studied, we did not do so on Barbados. Some people think that the island is too young to have participated in eustatic Quaternary changes of level, and they may be right. The question is still open, however, and will become a matter of serious investigation on our next trip.

The coral cap consists of ten or more steps that descend seaward as a flight of terraces. Each step inclines somewhat toward the coast. Sharp escarpments between them average nearly 100 feet high (Pl. 56). Except on the highest steps, rocks of the Oceanic Series are not ex-

PLATE 56. Escarpment separating two of the lower coral-cap terraces, near Six Men Bay, Barbados (Wyndover House shown in the picture). This was once a sea cliff.

PLATE 57. Lagoonal facies of coral-cap limestone, near River Bay, Barbados. Predominant among the organic specimens exposed on the 5-foot cliff are rodlike remains of staghorn coral.

posed on the surface. The cap has a thickness of about 260 feet, as shown both in caves at higher levels and in bore holes toward the coast. These interesting terraces, have been explained in many ways, but correctly in 1891 by Jukes-Browne and Harrison (1891 and 1892). No subsequent paper presents as much detail, acuteness in observation, or conceptual acumen. Harrison's work extended over something like ten years and he made excellent use of his time.

In eight main traverses that we made across the terraces we found in all cases that the escarpments separating them are capped by reef faunas dominated by elkhorn coral, living examples of which are shown in Plate 52. This is the conspicuous coral on slightly submerged reefs today and because of its massiveness serves as the most common source of lime for fertilizing the soils of volcanic islands such as Mauritius and Grenada. Behind the fossil reef crests there is a transition into faunas characteristic of lagoonal waters up to about forty feet deep (Pl. 57). Here, the more fragile staghorn coral is abundant. Living examples are shown in Plate 51. The evidence is clear that each terrace front is capped by a coral reef and that each flat behind contains reef-flat materials that gradually filled a lagoon (Skey, 1816). In several instances we found fossil patch reefs jutting up through the lagoonal deposits, each capped by limestone containing a shallow-water fauna (Pl. 58). Commonly we found examples of beach deposits on the inner sides of terraces. These were stratified and contained comminuted shells,

PLATE 58. Shallow-water fauna capping a patch reef near St. Thomas Church, Barbados.

some of which formed distinct, seaward-dipping layers. Although there was colluvial cover toward many escarpment bases, in a few cases we saw exposures of typical fore-reef sands inland and above fossil beaches, but below the shallow-water caps of scarp-top reefs. These exhibited comparatively good homogeneity and displayed types of cross bedding that are characteristic of fore-reef deposits today. Their content, presumably, runs high in fragments of *Halimeda* and plates of brittle stars. They are the local source of most building stones.

With the same sequence of facies on all terrace steps, it is evident that the Barbados terraces are depositional in origin, as explained by Jukes-Browne and Harrison. Were the relationships between land and sea that exist today uninterrupted for the next several thousand years, a new bench would be formed at low-tide level that would duplicate exactly the deposits and faunal facies present in each of the terraces.

The coral cap of Barbados indicates some ten or eleven periods when crustal stability permitted impressive reef-flat development, each of which was terminated by an uplift of the island that elevated the latest bench to a level where it became a terrace. The fore-reef slope suffered wave attacks sufficient to drive it back some distance and form a new sea cliff, but the process was soon checked by the growth of a new reef in water of appropriate depth and clearness some distance offshore. Massive coral structures are not likely to form in offshore waters on bottoms less than five or six fathoms deep because high waves move the bottom sand around too often to permit continuing attachment of coral secretions to a suitable substrate. Most active reefs around islands in the West Indies today appear to rise from a depth of less than ten fathoms. While this may have been true in the past, the reefs on Barbados were much thicker than this, probably because they grew while sea level was rising, a process that was slowed appreciably only 6,000 years ago, and that came almost to a halt some 3,000 years ago.

The amount of uplift experienced by the upper terraces in Barbados was considerably greater than their present elevations above sea level as they originated during sea stands that started some 450 feet lower and gradually decreased to the level at which today's reef is growing.

The uplifts that separate benches appear to have taken place during comparatively short periods separated by much longer times of relative tranquillity of the crust. The axis or center of most rapid uplift appears to have been located near the Scotland District of the eastern part of the island. Although bedrock of both the Scotland and Oceanic Series is readily erodible and is being degraded rapidly by sliding, slumping, and creep today, its presence at the summit of Mt. Hillaby is an adequate demonstration that uplift has been rapid.

Should uplift cease not more than a few centuries would be required to shift the culminating elevation of Barbados to the more resistant coral cap, some distance west of its present position. That the uplift is most rapid near the Scotland District is indicated by the fact that terrace surfaces are inclined seaward from there, mainly toward the west and southwest.

Some deformation of the coral cap has been experienced locally. Two minor anticlinal folds and several faults have been identified in the southern part of the island (Price, 1958). The main cliffs, however, are not fault scarps.

That the present is a time of crustal inactivity is indicated not only by reef relationships but also by the fact that Barbados has not experienced earthquakes recently. The island's seismographic station has recorded earthquakes from many other parts of the world but none of local origin. Barbados poses an extremely interesting geophysical question, "Why has intermittent uplift occurred during short time intervals separated by long periods of

crustal stability?" This question was raised in 1891 by
Jukes-Browne and Harrison.

Barbados also is interesting from the standpoint of its
karst topography. The limestone of its coral cap displays
at upper levels well-developed solution features such as
deep caves in which floors consist of Oceanic Series
rocks. Cane fields on higher terraces exhibit many deep
sink holes and almost vertically sided ravines. The topography is sufficiently rough that uncertainty exists as to
identification of one or more terrace surfaces at the top
of the flight. These modifications decrease in intensity on
lower members of the terrace sequence, but even on the
lowest surface there are displays of what I like to regard
as "flat karst," characterized by numerous more or less
round or oval-shaped lakes, ponds, or shallow sinks, such
as characterize many parts of the earth's surface. They
are conspicuous in the peninsula of Florida, across the
High Plains of Texas, where limestone lies not far below
the surface, and apparently on the Nullarbor Plain of
Western and South Australia (Jennings, 1963).

FUTURE OF PHYSICAL GEOGRAPHY

It has been my intention in presenting these Hitchcock
lectures to encourage the observation of interesting physical features that occur on all sides of us. Chance concentrated my own observations in flat areas and along sea
coasts, on problems that may not be solved completely
for many generations, but challenges of equal interest
are present on every kind of land surface. I regard geomorphology as an exciting science in its infancy, not as
one about which so much is known that it is profitable to
sit in an office engaging in the proposal of classifications
of land forms. Understanding of surface phenomena will
come from people with adequate training, interests, and
instincts of an explorer, who go into the field with enthusiasm. The ease with which one may get to most parts
of the world today and the advantages existing in meas-

urement and analytical techniques afford opportunities for making lasting contributions such as were denied investigators in the past. It is my personal hope that the "geo" remains in "geography," but if the proportion declines there will be no lesser need for studies of physical landscapes, and the requirement will be filled under some other disciplinary label, a matter of no great import if people continue researching the land surface, oceans, and atmosphere. It has been my good fortune to receive financial support from the Geography Branch of the Office of Naval Research for most of my travel and research. Undoubtedly support will be available from many sources to investigators for geomorphological studies for many decades and centuries to come. If the participants are adequately prepared and thoroughly enjoy their field work, the understanding of the earth's surface will become increasingly definitive, and the goals sought by William Morris Davis will become a reality.

REFERENCES

Davis, W. M.
    1928 The coral reef problem. Am. Geogr. Soc., Spec. Publ. 9, 596 pp.
Galloway, R. A. (see Krauss)
Harrison, J. B. (see Jukes-Browne)
Jennings, J. N.
    1963 Some geomorphological problems of the Nullarbor Plain. Roy. Soc. South Australia, Trans., 87:41–62.
Jukes-Browne, A. J.
    1891–1892 (with J. B. Harrison) The geology of Barbados. Geol. Soc. London, Quat. Jour. 47:179–249; 48:170–226.
Kaye, C. A.
    1959 Shoreline features and Quaternary shoreline changes, Puerto Rico. U. S. Geol. Surv., Prof. Paper 317:49–140.
Krauss, R. W.
    1960 (with R. A. Galloway) The role of algae in the formation of beach rock in certain islands of the Caribbean. La. State Univ., Coastal Studies Inst.,

Tech. Report 11, Part E, v + 49 pp. (available on microfilm, L. S. U. Library).

McIntire, W. G. (see Russell, 1965)

1961 Mauritius: river mouth terraces and present eustatic sea stand, in R. J. Russell (ed.), Pacific island terraces: eustatic? Zeit. f. Geomorphol., Supplementbd., 3:39–47.

Munk, W. H.

1948 (with M. C. Sargent) Adjustment of Bikini Atoll to ocean waves. Am. Geophys. Un., Trans., 29:855–860.

Price, E. T.

1958 Notes on the geography of Barbados. Tech. Rept., ONR contract 222(11) 388 067 with the Univ. of Calif., 60 pp.

Russell, R. J.

1959 Caribbean beach rock observations. Zeit. f. Geomorphol., 3:227–236.

1962 Origin of beach rock. Zeit. f. Geomorphol., 6:1–16.

1965 (with W. G. McIntire) Southern hemisphere beach rock. Geogr. Review 55:17–45.

Sargent, M. C. (see Munk)

Schuchert, C.

1935 Historical geology of the Antillean-Caribbean region, New York (John Wiley and Sons), 811 pp.

Skey, J.

1816 Some remarks upon the structure of Barbadoes, as connected with specimens of its rocks. Geol. Soc. London, Trans., 1816:236–242.

Wentworth, C. K.

1938–1939 Marine bench-forming processes. Jour. Geomorphol., 1:6–32; 2:3–25.

INDEX

(Boldface numbers refer to pages where either plates or figures appear.)

Abandoned channel, 74
Abbot, H. L., 5
Abrasion, sand, 129
Agassiz, L., 89
Agulhas, Cape, **87**
Ahlmann, H. W., 88
Albany, Western Australia, **86**
Algal: crusts, 125, 147; flats, 142 ff. **143, 146,** 153
Ak River, 56, 59
Alluvial cones, 31 ff., 56, 76; Lower Mississippi Valley, **32**; area, 34; vs. terraces, 34
Alluvial: fill, 23, 36; meandering, 64 ff.; morphology, 1 ff.
Alluviation, 10–11
Amazon: deltaic channels, **54,** 55
American school of geography, 2 ff.
Anabyssos, 133
Anastomosing (*see* Braided channels)
Anatolia, 55 ff.
Antarctic ice, 88
Antidunes, 113, **114**
Antigua, 93, 132, 133, 142, 157
Antilles: arcs, **156**; Lesser, 83, 139
Arizona, 92
Arkansas, river cone, 33
Artificial cut-offs, 76
Artificial levees, 72
Atchafalaya: basin, **10**; lake, **10**; river, 9, 63
Atolls, 90, 109, 137
Attalus Philadelphus, 104
Atwater, G. I., 13
Audrey, Hurricane, 97
Austausch (*see,* Turbulent exchange)
Australia (*see,* Darwin, Queensland, Western Australia)
Avery, Island, **78**
Aydin, 56

Backswamp, 48
Backwash, 101
Bafa, Lake, **58**
Bagnold, R. A., 100
Bank (*see* Caving); full, 29
Bar and swale topography, 67, **68**
Barbados, **143,** 156 ff., **157, 159, 160, 161**; geologic history, **158** ff.; karst, 164
Barbuda, 93, 142, **156** ff.
Bar-finger sands, 16
Bars (*see* Point Bar); marine, 101, 104
Base level, influence on coastal topography, 91
Baton Rouge 63; reach, **78,** 80
Beach, 83, 93 ff.; classification, 84; composition, 83, 94, 98, 162; cusps, 100; dune system, 106; long-straight, **99**; Louisiana, 95, 97–98; parts of, 100, **101**; Pleistocene, **94,** 137, 141; processes, 100 ff.; profiles, 99; sand, loss of, 104 ff.; shingle, 94–**95,** 96; steep, 99; study, detailed, 102, **103**; terminology, 100–101; types of, 93 ff., 99; variation in level, 93; winter, summer, 101, 106
Beach rock, 83 ff.; artifacts, 124–125; bands or pavements, 119, **120, 121, 122,** 134; cement, 127 ff., **131**; deformation, 135–136; exposure of, 123–124; origin, 124 ff., **133**; Pleistocene, 136, **137**; removal 132–133
Bed load, 47, 60, 66–67, 74
Bedrock: effect on shorelines, 85 ff.; planed, 92
Bed roughness, 113
Benches, 91 ff.
Bends, **69,** 70
Berms, 100